Kibana Essentials

Use the functionalities of Kibana to reveal insights from the data and build attractive visualizations and dashboards for real-world scenarios

Yuvraj Gupta

BIRMINGHAM - MUMBAI

Kibana Essentials

First published: October 2015

Production reference: 1261015

Published by Packt Publishing Ltd.
Livery Place
35 Livery Street
Birmingham B3 2PB, UK.

ISBN 978-1-78439-493-6

www.packtpub.com

Credits

Author
Yuvraj Gupta

Reviewers
Jacob Alves

Brent Ashley

David Laing

Commissioning Editor
Sarah Crofton

Acquisition Editor
Manish Nainani

Content Development Editor
Merwyn D'souza

Technical Editor
Shiny Poojary

Copy Editor
Vikrant Phadke

Project Coordinator
Neha Bhatnagar

Proofreader
Safis Editing

Indexer
Tejal Soni

Graphics
Disha Haria

Production Coordinator
Manu Joseph

Cover Work
Manu Joseph

About the Author

Yuvraj Gupta holds an undergraduate degree in computer science with a specialization in cloud computing and virtualization technology from UPES, Dehradun, India. He is currently working as a big data QA engineer. He has a keen interest in big data, data analytics, and visualization, and loves to try out new technologies.

Yuvraj is an avid gadget lover and makes it a point to stay up to date with the latest happenings in the technology domain. When he is not working, he spends his time on Facebook, Quora, and Stack Overflow, and also watches and plays sports. He can be reached at gupta.yuvraj@gmail.com or on LinkedIn at https://www.linkedin.com/in/guptayuvraj.

Acknowledgments

I had never thought of writing a technical book so soon in my life. It reminds me that opportunity knocks the door only once, and I am very lucky to have the opportunity of writing this book on the essentials of Kibana. However, ability is nothing without opportunity, and I would like to thank my acquisition editor, Manish Nainani, for scouting me and believing in a first-time author to write this book. I was lucky to have such an awesome content development editor, Merwyn D'Souza, who was very helpful and patient throughout the course of writing this book. In addition, I would like to thank the reviewers and the entire team of Packt Publishing, who were involved in producing this book. Without their support, it would never have been possible.

Special thanks to my dad, Sanjay, mom, Nisha, and brother, Adhiraj, for encouraging me and believing in me. I would also like to thank all my family members—Mamu, Massi, Massad, Taujis, Taijis, and my amazing cousins—for their blessings and guidance. A special shout out to all my friends, especially the cloud computing batch of 2015 and those who have helped me directly or indirectly in writing this book. Without everyone's support, I would have never been able to write this book.

I would also like to thank my teachers, professors, gurus, schools, and university for playing an important role in providing me with the education that has helped me gain knowledge.

Last but not least, I would like to extend my gratitude towards Elastic Inc. and Rashid for developing this awesome software with amazing features. This is a small contribution from my side to the ever-growing community of Kibana, and I hope this book helps Kibana reach greater heights.

About the Reviewers

Brent Ashley has been involved in computer technology and its surrounding communities since 1979, contributing via online forums, local and international events, papers, articles, and speeches.

As a leader and mentor in the development community, he became recognized in the early 2000s as an early pioneer in the web technologies that are now known as Ajax.

For more than 20 years, he worked as an Internet infrastructure architect and consultant, gaining extensive experience with networked asset configuration, management, monitoring, and log analysis.

Brent is the associate vice president of infrastructure architecture at ControlCase, LLC (`http://www.controlcase.com/`), a global innovator and leader in the provision and development of services, software products, hardware appliances, and managed solutions. The company focuses on compliance regulations and standards, including PCI DSS, ISO, SOX, HIPAA and many other regulatory environments and frameworks. Brent takes a lead role in the management and expansion of their international technology infrastructure as they continue to grow.

He was also a technical reviewer on the following books:

- *Foundations of Ajax*, Asleson and Schutta, *APress*, 2005
- *Enterprise Ajax*, Johnson, White, Charland, *Prentice Hall*, 2007

David Laing is a long-time member of the Cloud Foundry community. He is a core contributor to BOSH and the leader of the open source Logsearch (ELK + BOSH: `http://www.logsearch.io/`) project, which brings log analysis to the Cloud Foundry platform using ELK. David's company, stayUp.io (`http://www.stayup.io/`), provides commercial support for Logsearch.

www.PacktPub.com

Support files, eBooks, discount offers, and more

For support files and downloads related to your book, please visit www.PacktPub.com.

Did you know that Packt offers eBook versions of every book published, with PDF and ePub files available? You can upgrade to the eBook version at www.PacktPub.com and as a print book customer, you are entitled to a discount on the eBook copy. Get in touch with us at service@packtpub.com for more details.

At www.PacktPub.com, you can also read a collection of free technical articles, sign up for a range of free newsletters and receive exclusive discounts and offers on Packt books and eBooks.

https://www2.packtpub.com/books/subscription/packtlib

Do you need instant solutions to your IT questions? PacktLib is Packt's online digital book library. Here, you can search, access, and read Packt's entire library of books.

Why subscribe?

- Fully searchable across every book published by Packt
- Copy and paste, print, and bookmark content
- On demand and accessible via a web browser

Free access for Packt account holders

If you have an account with Packt at www.PacktPub.com, you can use this to access PacktLib today and view 9 entirely free books. Simply use your login credentials for immediate access.

This book is dedicated to my Nanu and Nani for motivating me and for being an inspiration to me.

Table of Contents

Preface

As big data has been trending in the industry for a while, huge amounts of data present a bigger challenge in gaining meaningful information from raw data. In today's industry, getting insights from data and making real-time decisions based on this huge data has become even more important.

Kibana provides an easy-to-use UI to perform real-time data analysis and visualizations on streaming data. It enables you to get hidden information by exploring data in different dimensions.

Making beautiful visualizations with ease without requiring any code and empowering people without technical knowledge to gather insights have never been easier.

What this book covers

Chapter 1, An Introduction to Kibana, takes you through the basic concepts of Elasticsearch, followed by the installation of Kibana and its prerequisite software.

Chapter 2, Exploring the Discover Page, covers the functionality of various components, along with detailed explanations of the usage of each component and its options.

Chapter 3, Exploring the Visualize Page, teaches you to create different types of visualizations using aggregations to visualize data.

Chapter 4, Exploring the Dashboard Page, covers the functionality of the various components present on the Dashboard page, followed by creating and embedding dashboards.

Chapter 5, Exploring the Settings Page, demonstrates the usage and tweaking of basic and advanced settings provided in Kibana.

Chapter 6, Real-Time Twitter Data Analysis, shows you how to analyze Twitter data and create visualizations based on different scenarios. This chapter also covers the workflow for analyzing Twitter data.

Appendix, References, contains a chapterwise segregation of the links and references used in the chapters.

What you need for this book

The following pieces of software are required:

- Oracle Java 1.8u20+
- Elasticsearch v1.4.4+
- A modern web browser—IE 10+, Firefox, Chrome, Safari, and so on
- Kibana v 4.1.1
- Git for Windows
- npm, Node.js, and elasticsearchdump for importing data in Elasticsearch
- Logstash v1.5.4

All of the software mentioned in this book is free of charge and can be downloaded from the Internet.

Who this book is for

Whether you are new to the world of data analytics and data visualization, or an expert, this book will provide you with the skills required to use Kibana for real-time visualization of streaming data with ease and simplicity. This book is intended for those professionals who are interested in learning about Kibana, about its installations, and how to use it. As Kibana provides a user-friendly web page, no prior experience is required.

Conventions

In this book, you will find a number of text styles that distinguish between different kinds of information. Here are some examples of these styles and an explanation of their meaning.

Code words in text, database table names, folder names, filenames, file extensions, pathnames, dummy URLs, user input, and Twitter handles are shown as follows: "Windows user can open the `elasticsearch.yml` file from the `config` folder."

A block of code is set as follows:

```
{
    "name": "Yuvraj",
    "age": 22,
    "birthdate": "2015-07-27",
    "bank_balance": 10500.50,
    "interests": ["playing games","movies","travelling"],
    "movie":
      {"name":"Titanic","genre":"Romance","year" : 1997}
}
```

Any command-line input or output is written as follows:

```
elasticdump \
--bulk=true \
--input="C:\Users\ygupta\Desktop\tweet.json" \
--output=http://localhost:9200/
```

Any hyperlink is written as follows:

```
https://github.com/guptayuvraj/Kibana_Essentials
```

New terms and **important words** are shown in bold. Words that you see on the screen, for example, in menus or dialog boxes, appear in the text like this: "Finally, click on **Create** to create the index in Kibana."

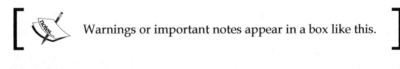
Warnings or important notes appear in a box like this.

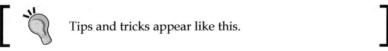
Tips and tricks appear like this.

Reader feedback

Feedback from our readers is always welcome. Let us know what you think about this book—what you liked or disliked. Reader feedback is important for us as it helps us develop titles that you will really get the most out of.

To send us general feedback, simply e-mail feedback@packtpub.com, and mention the book's title in the subject of your message.

If there is a topic that you have expertise in and you are interested in either writing or contributing to a book, see our author guide at www.packtpub.com/authors.

Customer support

Now that you are the proud owner of a Packt book, we have a number of things to help you to get the most from your purchase.

Downloading the color images of this book

We also provide you with a PDF file that has color images of the screenshots/ diagrams used in this book. The color images will help you better understand the changes in the output. You can download this file from https://www.packtpub. com/sites/default/files/downloads/4936OS_ColoredImages.pdf.

Errata

Although we have taken every care to ensure the accuracy of our content, mistakes do happen. If you find a mistake in one of our books—maybe a mistake in the text or the code—we would be grateful if you could report this to us. By doing so, you can save other readers from frustration and help us improve subsequent versions of this book. If you find any errata, please report them by visiting http://www.packtpub. com/submit-errata, selecting your book, clicking on the **Errata Submission Form** link, and entering the details of your errata. Once your errata are verified, your submission will be accepted and the errata will be uploaded to our website or added to any list of existing errata under the Errata section of that title.

To view the previously submitted errata, go to https://www.packtpub.com/books/ content/support and enter the name of the book in the search field. The required information will appear under the **Errata** section.

Piracy

Piracy of copyrighted material on the Internet is an ongoing problem across all media. At Packt, we take the protection of our copyright and licenses very seriously. If you come across any illegal copies of our works in any form on the Internet, please provide us with the location address or website name immediately so that we can pursue a remedy.

Please contact us at `copyright@packtpub.com` with a link to the suspected pirated material.

We appreciate your help in protecting our authors and our ability to bring you valuable content.

Questions

If you have a problem with any aspect of this book, you can contact us at `questions@packtpub.com`, and we will do our best to address the problem.

1
An Introduction to Kibana

Kibana is a tool that is part of the ELK stack, which consists of Elasticsearch, Logstash, and Kibana. It is built and developed by Elastic. Kibana is a visualization platform that is built on top of Elasticsearch and leverages the functionalities of Elasticsearch.

To understand Kibana better, let's check out the following diagram:

This diagram shows that Logstash is used to push data directly into Elasticsearch. This data is not limited to log data, but can include any type of data. Elasticsearch stores data that comes as input from Logstash, and Kibana uses the data stored in Elasticsearch to provide visualizations. So, Logstash provides an input stream of data to Elasticsearch, from which Kibana accesses the data and uses it to create visualizations.

Kibana acts as an over-the-top layer of Elasticsearch, providing beautiful visualizations for data (structured or nonstructured) stored in it. Kibana is an open source analytics product used to search, view, and analyze data. It provides various types of visualizations to visualize data in the form of tables, charts, maps, histograms, and so on. It also provides a web-based interface that can easily handle a large amount of data. It helps create dashboards that are easy to create and helps query data in real time. Dashboards are nothing but an interface for underlying JSON documents. They are used for saving, templating, and exporting. They are simple to set up and use, which helps us play with data stored in Elasticsearch in minutes without requiring any coding.

Kibana is an Apache-licensed product that aims to provide a flexible interface combined with the powerful searching capabilities of Elasticsearch. It requires a web server (included in the Kibana 4 package) and any modern web browser, that is, a browser that supports industry standards and renders the web page in the same way across all browsers, to work. It connects to Elasticsearch using the REST API. It helps to visualize data in real time with the use of dashboards to provide real-time insights.

In this book, we will use Kibana 4.1.1, which is the latest version of Kibana. It provides a lot of features compared to Kibana 3.

As Kibana uses the functionalities of Elasticsearch, it is easier to learn Kibana by understanding the core functionalities of Elasticsearch. In this chapter, we are going to take a look at the following topics:

- The basic concepts of Elasticsearch
- Installation of Java
- Installation of Elasticsearch
- Installation of Kibana
- Importing a JSON file into Elasticsearch

Understanding Elasticsearch

Elasticsearch is a search server built on top of Lucene (licensed under Apache), which is completely written in Java. It supports distributed searches in a multitenant environment. It is a scalable search engine allowing high flexibility of adding machines easily. It provides a full-text search engine combined with a RESTful web interface and JSON documents. Elasticsearch harnesses the functionalities of Lucene Java Libraries, adding up by providing proper APIs, scalability, and flexibility on top of the Lucene full-text search library. All querying done using Elasticsearch, that is, searching text, matching text, creating indexes, and so on, is implemented by Apache Lucene.

Without a setup of an Elastic shield or any other proxy mechanism, any user with access to Elasticsearch API can view all the data stored in the cluster.

The basic concepts of Elasticsearch

Let's explore some of the basic concepts of Elasticsearch:

- **Field**: This is the smallest single unit of data stored in Elasticsearch. It is similar to a column in a traditional relational database. Every document contains key-value pairs, which are referred to as fields. Values in a field can contain a single value, such as `integer [27]`, `string ["Kibana"]`, or multiple values, such as `array [1, 2, 3, 4, 5]`. The field type is responsible for specifying which type of data can be stored in a particular field, for example, `integer`, `string`, `date`, and so on.

- **Document**: This is the simplest unit of information stored in Elasticsearch. It is a collection of fields. It is considered similar to a row of a table in a traditional relational database. A document can contain any type of entry, such as a document for a single restaurant, another document for a single cuisine, and yet another for a single order. Documents are in **JavaScript Object Notation (JSON)**, which is a language-independent data interchange format. JSON contains key-value pairs. Every document that is stored in Elasticsearch is indexed. Every document contains a type and an ID. An example of a document that has JSON values is as follows:

```
{
    "name": "Yuvraj",
    "age": 22,
    "birthdate": "2015-07-27",
    "bank_balance": 10500.50,
    "interests": ["playing games","movies","travelling"],
    "movie": {"name":"Titanic","genre":"Romance","year" : 1997}
}
```

  In the preceding example, we can see that the document supports JSON, having key-value pairs, which are explained as follows:

  - The `name` field is of the string type
  - The `age` field is of the numeric type
  - The `birthdate` field is of the date type
  - The `bank_balance` field is of the float type
  - The `interests` field contains an array
  - The `movie` field contains an object (dictionary)

- **Type**: This is similar to a table in a traditional relational database. It contains a list of fields, which is defined for every document. A type is a logical segregation of indexes, whose interpretation/semantics entirely depends on you. For example, you have data about the world and you put all your data into an index. In this index, you can define a type for continent-wise data, another type for country-wise data, and a third type for region-wise data. Types are used with a mapping API; it specifies the type of its field. An example of type mapping is as follows:

```
{
  "user": {
    "properties": {
      "name": {
        "type": "string"
      },
      "age": {
        "type": "integer"
      },
      "birthdate": {
        "type": "date"
      },
      "bank_balance": {
        "type": "float"
      },
      "interests": {
        "type": "string"
      },
      "movie": {
        "properties": {
          "name": {
            "type": "string"
          },
          "genre": {
            "type": "string"
          },
          "year": {
            "type": "integer"
          }
        }
      }
    }
  }
}
```

Now, let's take a look at the core data types specified in Elasticsearch, as follows:

Type	Definition
string	This contains text, for example, "Kibana"
integer	This contains a 32-bit integer, for example, 7
long	This contains a 64-bit integer
float	IEEE float, for example, 2.7
double	This is a double-precision float
boolean	This can be true or false
date	This is the UTC date/time, for example, "2015-06-30T13:10:10"
geo_point	This is the latitude or longitude

- **Index**: This is a collection of documents (one or more than one). It is similar to a database in the analogy with traditional relational databases. For example, you can have an index for user information, transaction information, and product type. An index has a mapping; this mapping is used to define multiple types. In other words, an index can contain single or multiple types. An index is defined by a name, which is always used whenever referring to an index to perform search, update, and delete operations for documents. You can define any number of indexes you require. Indexes also act as logical namespaces that map documents to primary shards, which contain zero or more replica shards for replicating data. With respect to traditional databases, the basic analogy is similar to the following:

```
MySQL => Databases => Tables => Columns/Rows
Elasticsearch => Indexes => Types => Documents with Fields
```

> You can store a single document or multiple documents within a type or index. As a document is within an index, it must also be assigned to a type within an index. Moreover, the maximum number of documents that you can store in a single index is 2,147,483,519 (2 billion 147 million), which is equivalent to Integer.Max_Value.

- **ID**: This is an identifier for a document. It is used to identify each document. If it is not defined, it is autogenerated for every document.

> The combination of index, type, and ID must be unique for each document.

- **Mapping**: Mappings are similar to schemas in a traditional relational database. Every document in an index has a type. A mapping defines the fields, the data type for each field, and how the field should be handled by Elasticsearch. By default, a mapping is automatically generated whenever a document is indexed. If the default settings are overridden, then the mapping's definition has to be provided explicitly.

- **Node**: This is a running instance of Elasticsearch. Each node is part of a cluster. On a standalone machine, each Elasticsearch server instance corresponds to a node. Multiple nodes can be started on a single standalone machine or a single cluster. The node is responsible for storing data and helps in the indexing/searching capabilities of a cluster. By default, whenever a node is started, it is identified and assigned a random Marvel Comics character name. You can change the configuration file to name nodes as per your requirement. A node also needs to be configured in order to join a cluster, which is identifiable by the cluster name. By default, all nodes join the Elasticsearch cluster; that is, if any number of nodes are started up on a network/machine, they will automatically join the Elasticsearch cluster.

- **Cluster**: This is a collection of nodes and has one or multiple nodes; they share a single cluster name. Each cluster automatically chooses a master node, which is replaced if it fails; that is, if the master node fails, another random node will be chosen as the new master node, thus providing high availability. The cluster is responsible for holding all of the data stored and provides a unified view for search capabilities across all nodes. By default, the cluster name is Elasticsearch, and it is the identifiable parameter for all nodes in a cluster. All nodes, by default, join the Elasticsearch cluster. While using a cluster in the production phase, it is advisable to change the cluster name for ease of identification, but the default name can be used for any other purpose, such as development or testing.

 The Elasticsearch cluster contains single or multiple indexes, which contain single or multiple types. All types contain single or multiple documents, and every document contains single or multiple fields.

- **Sharding**: This is an important concept of Elasticsearch while understanding how Elasticsearch allows scaling of nodes, when having a large amount of data termed as big data. An index can store any amount of data, but if it exceeds its disk limit, then searching would become slow and be affected. For example, the disk limit is 1 TB, and an index contains a large number of documents, which may not fit completely within 1 TB in a single node. To counter such problems, Elasticsearch provides shards. These break the index into multiple pieces. Each shard acts as an independent index that is hosted on a node within a cluster. Elasticsearch is responsible for distributing shards among nodes. There are two purposes of sharding: allowing horizontal scaling of the content volume, and improving performance by providing parallel operations across various shards that are distributed on nodes (single or multiple, depending on the number of nodes running).

> Elasticsearch helps move shards among multiple nodes in the event of an addition of new nodes or a node failure.

There are two types of shards, as follows:

- **Primary shard**: Every document is stored within a primary index. By default, every index has five primary shards. This parameter is configurable and can be changed to define more or fewer shards as per the requirement. A primary shard has to be defined before the creation of an index. If no parameters are defined, then five primary shards will automatically be created.

> Whenever a document is indexed, it is usually done on a primary shard initially, followed by replicas. The number of primary shards defined in an index cannot be altered once the index is created.

○ **Replica shard**: Replica shards are an important feature of Elasticsearch. They help provide high availability across nodes in the cluster. By default, every primary shard has one replica shard. However, every primary shard can have zero or more replica shards as required. In an environment where failure directly affects the enterprise, it is highly recommended to use a system that provides a failover mechanism to achieve high availability. To counter this problem, Elasticsearch provides a mechanism in which it creates single or multiple copies of indexes, and these are termed as replica shards or replicas. A replica shard is a full copy of the primary shard. Replica shards can be dynamically altered. Now, let's see the purposes of creating a replica. It provides high availability in the event of failure of a node or a primary shard. If there is a failure of a primary shard, replica shards are automatically promoted to primary shards. Increase performance by providing parallel operations on replica shards to handle search requests.

 A replica shard is never kept on the same node as that of the primary shard from which it was copied.

• **Inverted index**: This is also a very important concept in Elasticsearch. It is used to provide fast full-text search. Instead of searching text, it searches for an index. It creates an index that lists unique words occurring in a document, along with the document list in which each word occurs. For example, suppose we have three documents. They have a text field, and it contains the following:

○ I am learning Kibana

○ Kibana is an amazing product

○ Kibana is easy to use

To create an inverted index, the text field is broken into words (also known as terms), a list of unique words is created, and also a listing is done of the document in which the term occurs, as shown in this table:

Term	Doc 1	Doc 2	Doc 3
I	X		
Am	X		
Learning	X		
Kibana	X	X	X
Is		X	X
An		X	

Term	Doc 1	Doc 2	Doc 3
Amazing		X	
Product		X	
Easy			X
To			X
Use			X

Now, if we search for is Kibana, Elasticsearch will use an inverted index to display the results:

Term	Doc 1	Doc 2	Doc 3
Is		X	X
Kibana	X	X	X

With inverted indexes, Elasticsearch uses the functionality of Lucene to provide fast full-text search results.

 An inverted index uses an index based on keywords (terms) instead of a document-based index.

- **REST API**: This stands for **Representational State Transfer**. It is a stateless client-server protocol that uses HTTP requests to store, view, and delete data. It supports **CRUD** operations (short for **Create, Read, Update, and Delete**) using HTTP. It is used to communicate with Elasticsearch and is implemented by all languages. It communicates with Elasticsearch over port 9200 (by default), which is accessible from any web browser. Also, Elasticsearch can be directly communicated with via the command line using the curl command. **cURL** is a command-line tool used to send, view, or delete data using URL syntax, as followed by the HTTP structure. A cURL request is similar to an HTTP request, which is as follows:

```
curl -X <VERB> '<PROTOCOL>://<HOSTNAME>:<PORT>/<PATH>?<QUERY_
STRING>' -d '<BODY>'
```

The terms marked within the <> tags are variables, which are defined as follows:

  ° **VERB**: This is used to provide an appropriate HTTP method, such as GET (to get data), POST, PUT (to store data), or DELETE (to delete data).

- ° **PROTOCOL**: This is used to define whether the HTTP or HTTPS protocol is used to send requests.
- ° **HOSTNAME**: This is used to define the hostname of a node present in the Elasticsearch cluster. By default, the hostname of Elasticsearch is `localhost`.
- ° **PORT**: This is used to define the port on which Elasticsearch is running. By default, Elasticsearch runs on port `9200`.
- ° **PATH**: This is used to define the index, type, and ID where the documents will be stored, searched, or deleted. It is specified as index/type/ID.
- ° **QUERY_STRING**: This is used to define any additional query parameter for searching data.
- ° **BODY**: This is used to define a JSON-encoded request within the body.

In order to put data into Elasticsearch, the following `curl` command is used:

```
curl -XPUT 'http://localhost:9200/testing/test/1' -d '{"name":
"Kibana" }'
```

Here, `testing` is the name of the index, `test` is the name of the type within the index, and `1` indicates the ID number.

To search for the preceding stored data, the following `curl` command is used:

```
curl -XGET 'http://localhost:9200/testing/_search?
```

 The preceding commands are provided just to give you an overview of the format of the `curl` command.

Prerequisites for installing Kibana 4.1.1

The following pieces of software need to be installed before installing Kibana 4.1.1:

- Java 1.8u20+
- Elasticsearch v1.4.4+
- A modern web browser—IE 10+, Firefox, Chrome, Safari, and so on

The installation process will be covered separately for Windows and Ubuntu so that both types of users are able to understand the process of installation easily.

Installation of Java

In this section, JDK needs to be installed so as to access Elasticsearch. Oracle Java 8 (update 20 onwards) will be installed as it is the recommended version for Elasticsearch from version 1.4.4 onwards.

Installation of Java on Ubuntu 14.04

Install Java 8 using the terminal and the apt package in the following manner:

1. Add the Oracle Java **Personal Package Archive (PPA)** to the `apt` repository list:

    ```
    sudo add-apt-repository -y ppa:webupd8team/java
    ```

    ```
    yuvraj@L212:~$ sudo add-apt-repository -y ppa:webupd8team/java
    [sudo] password for yuvraj:
    gpg: keyring '/tmp/tmpcx59wizk/secring.gpg' created
    gpg: keyring '/tmp/tmpcx59wizk/pubring.gpg' created
    gpg: requesting key EEA14886 from hkp server keyserver.ubuntu.com
    gpg: /tmp/tmpcx59wizk/trustdb.gpg: trustdb created
    gpg: key EEA14886: public key "Launchpad VLC" imported
    gpg: Total number processed: 1
    gpg:               imported: 1  (RSA: 1)
    OK
    ```

 In this case, we use a third-party repository; however, the WebUpd8 team is trusted to install Java. It does not include any Java binaries. Instead, the PPA directly downloads from Oracle and installs it.

As shown in the preceding screenshot, you will initially be prompted for the password for running the `sudo` command (only when you have not logged in as root), and on successful addition to the repository, you will receive an OK message, which means that the repository has been imported.

2. Update the `apt` package database to include all the latest files under the packages:

```
sudo apt-get update
```

```
Get:27 http://in.archive.ubuntu.com trusty-updates/restricted amd64 Packages [11.8 kB]
Get:28 http://in.archive.ubuntu.com trusty-updates/universe amd64 Packages [284 kB]
Get:29 http://in.archive.ubuntu.com trusty-updates/multiverse amd64 Packages [11.9 kB]
Get:30 http://in.archive.ubuntu.com trusty-updates/main i386 Packages [519 kB]
Get:31 http://in.archive.ubuntu.com trusty-updates/restricted i386 Packages [11.8 kB]
Get:32 http://in.archive.ubuntu.com trusty-updates/universe i386 Packages [285 kB]
Get:33 http://in.archive.ubuntu.com trusty-updates/multiverse i386 Packages [12.1 kB]
Hit http://in.archive.ubuntu.com trusty-updates/main Translation-en
Hit http://in.archive.ubuntu.com trusty-updates/multiverse Translation-en
Hit http://in.archive.ubuntu.com trusty-updates/restricted Translation-en
Hit http://in.archive.ubuntu.com trusty-updates/universe Translation-en
Hit http://in.archive.ubuntu.com trusty-backports/main Sources
Hit http://in.archive.ubuntu.com trusty-backports/restricted Sources
Hit http://in.archive.ubuntu.com trusty-backports/universe Sources
Hit http://in.archive.ubuntu.com trusty-backports/multiverse Sources
Hit http://in.archive.ubuntu.com trusty-backports/main amd64 Packages
Hit http://in.archive.ubuntu.com trusty-backports/restricted amd64 Packages
Hit http://in.archive.ubuntu.com trusty-backports/universe amd64 Packages
Hit http://in.archive.ubuntu.com trusty-backports/multiverse amd64 Packages
Hit http://in.archive.ubuntu.com trusty-backports/main i386 Packages
Hit http://in.archive.ubuntu.com trusty-backports/restricted i386 Packages
Hit http://in.archive.ubuntu.com trusty-backports/universe i386 Packages
Hit http://in.archive.ubuntu.com trusty-backports/multiverse i386 Packages
Hit http://in.archive.ubuntu.com trusty-backports/main Translation-en
Hit http://in.archive.ubuntu.com trusty-backports/multiverse Translation-en
Hit http://in.archive.ubuntu.com trusty-backports/restricted Translation-en
Hit http://in.archive.ubuntu.com trusty-backports/universe Translation-en
Ign http://in.archive.ubuntu.com trusty/main Translation-en_IN
Ign http://in.archive.ubuntu.com trusty/multiverse Translation-en_IN
Ign http://in.archive.ubuntu.com trusty/restricted Translation-en_IN
Ign http://in.archive.ubuntu.com trusty/universe Translation-en_IN
Fetched 3,059 kB in 26s (116 kB/s)
Reading package lists... Done
```

3. Install the latest version of Oracle Java 8:

```
sudo apt-get -y install oracle-java8-installer
```

```
yuvraj@L212:~$ sudo apt-get -y install oracle-java8-installer
Reading package lists... Done
Building dependency tree
Reading state information... Done
The following packages were automatically installed and are no longer required:
  libunibreak1 libzlcore-data libzlcore0.12 libzltext-data libzltext0.12
  libzlui-qt4
Use 'apt-get autoremove' to remove them.
Suggested packages:
  binfmt-support visualvm ttf-baekmuk ttf-unfonts ttf-unfonts-core
  ttf-kochi-gothic ttf-sazanami-gothic ttf-kochi-mincho ttf-sazanami-mincho
  ttf-arphic-uming
The following NEW packages will be installed:
  oracle-java8-installer
0 upgraded, 1 newly installed, 0 to remove and 436 not upgraded.
Need to get 0 B/22.6 kB of archives.
After this operation, 129 kB of additional disk space will be used.
Preconfiguring packages ...
Selecting previously unselected package oracle-java8-installer.
(Reading database ... 179955 files and directories currently installed.)
Preparing to unpack .../oracle-java8-installer_8u45+8u33arm-1~webupd8-1_all.deb ...
oracle-license-v1-1 license has already been accepted
Unpacking oracle-java8-installer (8u45+8u33arm-1~webupd8-1) ...
Processing triggers for gnome-menus (3.10.1-0ubuntu2) ...
Processing triggers for desktop-file-utils (0.22-1ubuntu1) ...
Processing triggers for bamfdaemon (0.5.1+14.04.20140409-0ubuntu1) ...
Rebuilding /usr/share/applications/bamf-2.index...
Processing triggers for mime-support (3.54ubuntu1) ...
Processing triggers for shared-mime-info (1.2-0ubuntu3) ...
```

Also, during the installation, you will be prompted to accept the license agreement, which pops up as follows:

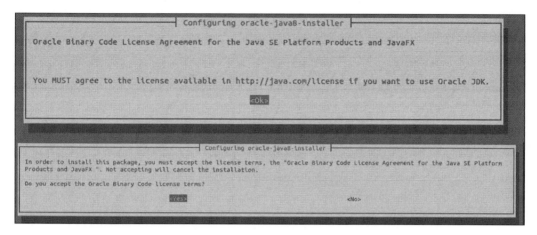

4. To check whether Java has been successfully installed, type the following command in the terminal:

```
java -version
```

```
yuvraj@L212:~$ java -version
java version "1.8.0_45"
Java(TM) SE Runtime Environment (build 1.8.0_45-b14)
Java HotSpot(TM) 64-Bit Server VM (build 25.45-b02, mixed mode)
```

This signifies that Java has been installed successfully.

Installation of Java on Windows

We can install Java on windows by going through the following steps:

1. Download the latest version of the Java JDK from the Sun Microsystems
    site at `http://www.oracle.com/technetwork/java/javase/downloads/`
    `index.html`:

2. As shown in the preceding screenshot, click on the **DOWNLOAD** button of
    JDK to download. You will be redirected to the download page. There, you
    have to first click on the **Accept License Agreement** radio button, followed
    by the Windows version to download the `.exe` file, as shown here:

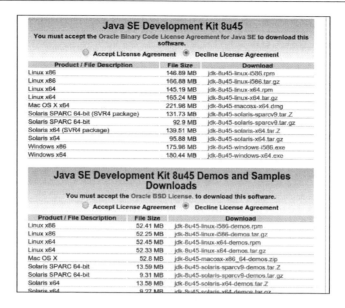

3. Double-click on the file to be installed and it will open as an installer.

4. Click on **Next**, accept the license by reading it, and keep clicking on **Next** until it shows that JDK has been installed successfully.

5. Now, to run Java on Windows, you need to set the path of JAVA in the environment variable settings of Windows. Firstly, open the properties of **My Computer**. Select the **Advanced** system settings and then click on the **Advanced** tab, wherein you have to click on the environment variables option, as shown in this screenshot:

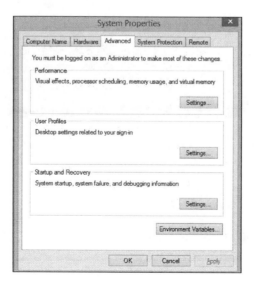

After opening **Environment Variables**, click on **New** (under the **System** variables) and give the variable name as JAVA_HOME and variable value as C:\Program Files\Java\jdk1.8.0_45 (do check in your system where jdk has been installed and provide the path corresponding to the version installed as mentioned in system directory), as shown in the following screenshot:

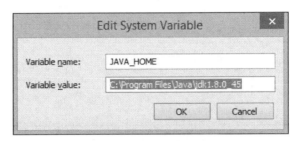

Then, double-click on the **Path** variable (under the **System** variables) and move towards the end of textbox. Insert a semicolon if it is not already inserted, and add the location of the bin folder of JDK, like this: %JAVA_HOME%\bin. Next, click on **OK** in all the windows opened.

 Do not delete anything within the path variable textbox.

6. To check whether Java is installed or not, type the following command in Command Prompt:

```
java -version
```

This signifies that Java has been installed successfully.

Installation of Elasticsearch

In this section, Elasticsearch, which is required to access Kibana, will be installed. Elasticsearch v1.5.2 will be installed, and this section covers the installation on Ubuntu and Windows separately.

Installation of Elasticsearch on Ubuntu 14.04

To install Elasticsearch on Ubuntu, perform the following steps:

1. Download Elasticsearch v 1.5.2 as a `.tar` file using the following command on the terminal:

   ```
   curl -L -O https://download.elastic.co/elasticsearch/
   elasticsearch/elasticsearch-1.5.2.tar.gz
   ```

   ```
   yuvraj@L212:~$ curl -L -O https://download.elastic.co/elasticsearch/elasticsearch/elasticsearch-1.5.2.tar.gz
     % Total    % Received % Xferd  Average Speed   Time    Time     Time  Current
                                    Dload  Upload   Total   Spent    Left  Speed
   100 26.8M  100 26.8M    0     0   432k      0  0:01:03  0:01:03 --:--:-- 1043k
   ```

    Curl is a package that may not be installed on Ubuntu by the user. To use curl, you need to install the curl package, which can be done using the following command:

   ```
   sudo apt-get -y install curl
   ```

2. Extract the downloaded `.tar` file using this command:

   ```
   tar -xvzf elasticsearch-1.5.2.tar.gz
   ```

   This will extract the files and folder into the current working directory.

3. Navigate to the `bin` directory within the `elasticsearch-1.5.2` directory:

   ```
   cd elasticsearch-1.5.2/bin
   ```

4. Now run Elasticsearch to start the node and cluster, using the following command:

   ```
   ./elasticsearch
   ```

   ```
   yuvraj@L212:~/elasticsearch-1.5.2/bin$ ./elasticsearch
   [2015-06-11 15:16:56,261][INFO ][node            ] [Fan Boy] version[1.5.2], pid[26804], build[62ff986/2015-04-27T09:21:06Z]
   [2015-06-11 15:16:56,262][INFO ][node            ] [Fan Boy] initializing ...
   [2015-06-11 15:16:56,267][INFO ][plugins         ] [Fan Boy] loaded [], sites []
   [2015-06-11 15:16:59,417][INFO ][node            ] [Fan Boy] initialized
   [2015-06-11 15:16:59,418][INFO ][node            ] [Fan Boy] starting ...
   [2015-06-11 15:16:59,551][INFO ][transport       ] [Fan Boy] bound_address {inet[/0:0:0:0:0:0:0:0:9300]}, publish_address {inet[/172.16
   .0.93:9300]}
   [2015-06-11 15:16:59,692][INFO ][discovery       ] [Fan Boy] elasticsearch/JUCiUHVQSS6PBlesY3ENaA
   [2015-06-11 15:17:03,507][INFO ][cluster.service ] [Fan Boy] new_master [Fan Boy][JUCiUHVQSS6PBlesY3ENaA][L212][inet[/172.16.0.93:9300]
   ], reason: zen-disco-join (elected_as_master)
   [2015-06-11 15:17:03,554][INFO ][http            ] [Fan Boy] bound_address {inet[/0:0:0:0:0:0:0:0:9200]}, publish_address {inet[/172.16
   .0.93:9200]}
   [2015-06-11 15:17:03,555][INFO ][node            ] [Fan Boy] started
   [2015-06-11 15:17:03,636][INFO ][gateway         ] [Fan Boy] recovered [0] indices into cluster_state
   ```

   The preceding screenshot shows that the Elasticsearch node has been started, and it has been given a random Marvel Comics character name.

If this terminal is closed, Elasticsearch will stop running as this node will shut down. However, if you have multiple Elasticsearch nodes running, then shutting down a node will not result in shutting down Elasticsearch.

5. To verify the Elasticsearch installation, open `http://localhost:9200` in your browser.

```
{
  "status" : 200,
  "name" : "Fan Boy",
  "cluster_name" : "elasticsearch",
  "version" : {
    "number" : "1.5.2",
    "build_hash" : "62ff9868b4c8a0c45860bebb259e21980778ab1c",
    "build_timestamp" : "2015-04-27T09:21:06Z",
    "build_snapshot" : false,
    "lucene_version" : "4.10.4"
  },
  "tagline" : "You Know, for Search"
}
```

Installation of Elasticsearch on Windows

The installation on Windows can be done by following similar steps as in the case of Ubuntu. To use `curl` commands on Windows, we will be installing GIT. GIT will also be used to import a sample JSON file into Elasticsearch using `elasticdump`, as described in the *Importing a JSON file into Elasticsearch* section.

Installation of GIT

To run `curl` commands on Windows, first download and install GIT, then perform the following steps:

1. Download the GIT ZIP package from `https://git-scm.com/download/win`.

2. Double-click on the downloaded file, which will walk you through the installation process.

3. Keep clicking on **Next** by not changing the default options until the **Finish** button is clicked on.

4. To validate the GIT installation, right-click on any folder in which you should be able to see the options of GIT, such as **GIT Bash**, as shown in the following screenshot:

The following are the steps required to install Elasticsearch on Windows:

1. Open **GIT Bash** and enter the following command in the terminal:

   ```
   curl -L -O https://download.elastic.co/elasticsearch/
   elasticsearch/elasticsearch-1.5.2.zip
   ```

   ```
   ygupta@XE-T-YGUPTA /C/Users/ygupta/Desktop/Personal
   $ curl -L -O https://download.elastic.co/elasticsearch/elasticsearch/elasticsea
   rch-1.5.2.zip
     % Total    % Received % Xferd  Average Speed   Time    Time     Time  Current
                                    Dload  Upload   Total   Spent    Left  Speed
     1 29.9M    1  319k    0     0   6252      0  1:23:47  0:00:52  1:22:55  9648
   ```

2. Extract the downloaded ZIP package by either unzipping it using WinRar, 7Zip, and so on (if you don't have any of these, download one of them) or using the following command in **GIT Bash**:

   ```
   unzip elasticsearch-1.5.2.zip
   ```

   This will extract the files and folder into the directory.

3. Then click on the extracted folder and navigate through it to reach the `bin` folder.

4. Click on the `elasticsearch.bat` file to run Elasticsearch.

```
Elasticsearch 1.5.2                                             _ □ x
[2015-06-27 11:43:26,708][INFO ][node                     ] [Astronomer] version
[1.5.2], pid[4700], build[62ff986/2015-04-27T09:21:06Z]
[2015-06-27 11:43:26,716][INFO ][node                     ] [Astronomer] initial
izing ...
[2015-06-27 11:43:26,813][INFO ][plugins                  ] [Astronomer] loaded
[river-twitter], sites [head]
[2015-06-27 11:43:30,192][INFO ][node                     ] [Astronomer] initial
ized
[2015-06-27 11:43:39,290][INFO ][node                     ] [Astronomer] startin
g ...
[2015-06-27 11:43:39,661][INFO ][transport                ] [Astronomer] bound_a
ddress {inet[/0:0:0:0:0:0:0:0:9300]}, publish_address {inet[/192.168.1.111:9300]
}
[2015-06-27 11:43:39,887][INFO ][discovery                ] [Astronomer] elastic
search/QgQrCrAySDaKQpøm2sAg7A
[2015-06-27 11:43:43,692][INFO ][cluster.service          ] [Astronomer] new_mas
ter [Astronomer][QgQrCrAySDaKQpøm2sAg7A][XE-T-YGUPTA][inet[/192.168.1.111:9300]]
, reason: zen-disco-join (elected_as_master)
[2015-06-27 11:43:43,838][INFO ][http                     ] [Astronomer] bound_a
ddress {inet[/0:0:0:0:0:0:0:0:9200]}, publish_address {inet[/192.168.1.111:9200]
}
[2015-06-27 11:43:43,838][INFO ][node                     ] [Astronomer] started
```

The preceding screenshot shows that the Elasticsearch node has been started, and it is given a random Marvel Comics character's name.

> Again, if this window is closed, Elasticsearch will stop running as this node will shut down. However, if you have multiple Elasticsearch nodes running, then shutting down a node will not result in shutting down Elasticsearch.

5. To verify the Elasticsearch installation, open `http://localhost:9200` in your browser.

```
{
  "status" : 200,
  "name" : "Astronomer",
  "cluster_name" : "elasticsearch",
  "version" : {
    "number" : "1.5.2",
    "build_hash" : "62ff9868b4c8a0c45860bebb259e21980778ab1c",
    "build_timestamp" : "2015-04-27T09:21:06Z",
    "build_snapshot" : false,
    "lucene_version" : "4.10.4"
  },
  "tagline" : "You Know, for Search"
}
```

Installation of Kibana

In this section, Kibana will be installed. We will install Kibana v4.1.1, and this section covers installations on Ubuntu and Windows separately.

Installation of Kibana on Ubuntu 14.04

To install Kibana on Ubuntu, follow these steps:

1. Download Kibana version 4.1.1 as a `.tar` file using the following command in the terminal:

```
curl -L -O https://download.elasticsearch.org/kibana/kibana/
kibana-4.1.1-linux-x64.tar.gz
```

```
yuvraj@L212:~$ curl -L -O https://download.elasticsearch.org/kibana/kibana/kibana-4.1.1-linux-x64.tar.gz
  % Total    % Received % Xferd  Average Speed   Time    Time     Time  Current
                                 Dload  Upload   Total   Spent    Left  Speed
100 11.1M  100 11.1M    0     0   520k      0  0:00:21  0:00:21 --:--:--  622k
```

2. Extract the downloaded `.tar` file using this command:

```
tar -xvzf kibana-4.1.1-linux-x64.tar.gz
```

The preceding command will extract the files and folder into the current working directory.

3. Navigate to the `bin` directory within the `kibana-4.1.1-linux-x64` directory:

```
cd kibana-4.1.1-linux-x64/bin
```

4. Now run Kibana to start the node and cluster using the following command:

```
./kibana
```

```
yuvraj@L212:~$ cd kibana-4.1.1-linux-x64/bin/
yuvraj@L212:~/kibana-4.1.1-linux-x64/bin$ ./kibana
{"name":"Kibana","hostname":"L212","pid":25104,"level":30,"msg":"Found kibana index","time":"2015-09-26T16:00:05.889Z","v":0}
{"name":"Kibana","hostname":"L212","pid":25104,"level":30,"msg":"Listening on 0.0.0.0:5601","time":"2015-09-26T16:00:06.123Z","v":0}
```

Make sure that Elasticsearch is running. If it is not running and you try to start Kibana, the following error will be displayed after you run the preceding command:

```
yuvraj@L212:~/kibana-4.1.1-linux-x64/bin$ ./kibana
{"name":"Kibana","hostname":"L212","pid":25145,"level":50,"err":"Request error, retrying -- connect ECONNREFUSED","msg":"","time":"2015-09-26T16:00:23.105Z","v":0}
{"name":"Kibana","hostname":"L212","pid":25145,"level":40,"msg":"Unable to revive connection: http://localhost:9200/","time":"2015-09-26T16:00:23.110Z","v":0}
{"name":"Kibana","hostname":"L212","pid":25145,"level":40,"msg":"No living connections","time":"2015-09-26T16:00:23.110Z","v":0}
{"name":"Kibana","hostname":"L212","pid":25145,"level":30,"msg":"Unable to connect to elasticsearch at http://localhost:9200. Retrying in 2.5 seconds.","time":"2015-09-26T16:00:23.113Z","v":0}
```

5. To verify the Kibana installation, open `http://localhost:5601` in your browser.

Installation of Kibana on Windows

To install Kibana on Windows, perform the following steps:

1. Open **GIT Bash** and enter the following command in the terminal:

```
curl -L -O https://download.elasticsearch.org/kibana/kibana/
kibana-4.1.1-windows.zip
```

```
ygupta@XE-T-YGUPTA /C/Users/ygupta/Desktop
$ curl -L -O https://download.elasticsearch.org/kibana/kibana/kibana-4.1.1-wind
ows.zip
  % Total    % Received % Xferd  Average Speed   Time    Time     Time  Current
                                 Dload  Upload   Total   Spent    Left  Speed
 16 10.0M   16 1663k    0     0   110k      0  0:01:33  0:00:15  0:01:18  121k
```

2. Extract the downloaded ZIP package by either unzipping it using WinRar or 7Zip (download it if you don't have it), or using the following command in **GIT Bash**:

```
unzip kibana-4.1.1-windows.zip
```

This will extract the files and folder into the directory.

3. Then click on the extracted folder and navigate through it to get to the `bin` folder.

4. Click on the `kibana.bat` file to run Kibana.

> Make sure that Elasticsearch is running. If it is not running and you try to start Kibana, the following error will be displayed after you click on the `kibana.bat` file:

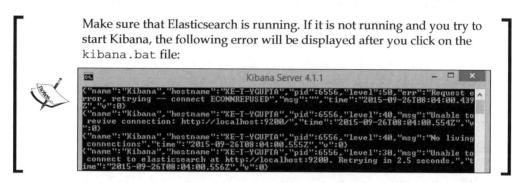

5. Again, to verify the Kibana installation, open `http://localhost:5601` in your browser.

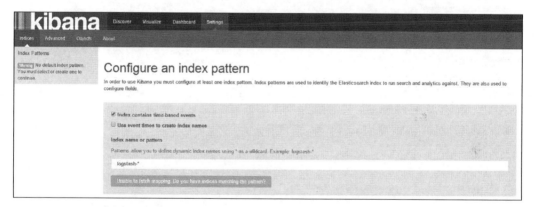

Additional information

You can change the Elasticsearch configuration for your production environment, wherein you have to change parameters such as the cluster name, node name, network address, and so on. This can be done using the information mentioned in the upcoming sections.

Changing the Elasticsearch configuration

To change the Elasticsearch configuration, perform the following steps:

1. Run the following command in the terminal to open the configuration file:

   ```
   sudo vi ~/elasticsearch-1.5.2/config/elasticsearch.yml
   ```

   Windows users can open the elasticsearch.yml file from the config
   folder. This will open the configuration file as follows:

```
#################### Elasticsearch Configuration Example ####################

# This file contains an overview of various configuration settings,
# targeted at operations staff. Application developers should
# consult the guide at <http://elasticsearch.org/guide>.
#
# The installation procedure is covered at
# <http://elasticsearch.org/guide/en/elasticsearch/reference/current/setup.html>.
#
# Elasticsearch comes with reasonable defaults for most settings,
# so you can try it out without bothering with configuration.
#
# Most of the time, these defaults are just fine for running a production
# cluster. If you're fine-tuning your cluster, or wondering about the
# effect of certain configuration option, please _do ask_ on the
# mailing list or IRC channel [http://elasticsearch.org/community].

# Any element in the configuration can be replaced with environment variables
# by placing them in ${...} notation. For example:
#
#node.rack: ${RACK_ENV_VAR}

# For information on supported formats and syntax for the config file, see
# <http://elasticsearch.org/guide/en/elasticsearch/reference/current/setup-configuration.html>


################################### Cluster ###################################

# Cluster name identifies your cluster for auto-discovery. If you're running
# multiple clusters on the same network, make sure you're using unique names.
#
#cluster.name: elasticsearch


#################################### Node ####################################

# Node names are generated dynamically on startup, so you're relieved
# from configuring them manually. You can tie this node to a specific name:
#
#node.name: "Franz Kafka"
"elasticsearch-1.5.2/config/elasticsearch.yml" 385 lines, 13476 characters
```

2. The cluster name can be changed, as follows:

   `#cluster.name: elasticsearch to cluster.name: "your_cluster_name"`.

```
####################### Elasticsearch Configuration Example #####################

# This file contains an overview of various configuration settings,
# targeted at operations staff. Application developers should
# consult the guide at <http://elasticsearch.org/guide>.
#
# The installation procedure is covered at
# <http://elasticsearch.org/guide/en/elasticsearch/reference/current/setup.html>.
#
# Elasticsearch comes with reasonable defaults for most settings,
# so you can try it out without bothering with configuration.
#
# Most of the time, these defaults are just fine for running a production
# cluster. If you're fine-tuning your cluster, or wondering about the
# effect of certain configuration option, please _do ask_ on the
# mailing list or IRC channel [http://elasticsearch.org/community].
#
# Any element in the configuration can be replaced with environment variables
# by placing them in ${...} notation. For example:
#
#node.rack: ${RACK_ENV_VAR}

# For information on supported formats and syntax for the config file, see
# <http://elasticsearch.org/guide/en/elasticsearch/reference/current/setup-configuration.html>


################################## Cluster ###################################

# Cluster name identifies your cluster for auto-discovery. If you're running
# multiple clusters on the same network, make sure you're using unique names.
#
cluster.name: test


#################################### Node ####################################

# Node names are generated dynamically on startup, so you're relieved
# from configuring them manually. You can tie this node to a specific name:
#
#node.name: "Franz Kafka"
"~/elasticsearch-1.5.2/config/elasticsearch.yml" 385 lines, 13466 characters
```

In the preceding figure, the cluster name has been changed to `test`. Then, we save the file.

3. To verify that the cluster name has been changed, run Elasticsearch as mentioned in the earlier section.

Then open `http://localhost:9200` in the browser to verify, as shown here:

```
{
  "status" : 200,
  "name" : "Slick",
  "cluster_name" : "test",
  "version" : {
    "number" : "1.5.2",
    "build_hash" : "62ff9868b4c8a0c45860bebb259e21980778ab1c",
    "build_timestamp" : "2015-04-27T09:21:06Z",
    "build_snapshot" : false,
    "lucene_version" : "4.10.4"
  },
  "tagline" : "You Know, for Search"
}
```

In the preceding screenshot, you can notice that `cluster_name` has been changed to `test`, as specified earlier.

Changing the Kibana configuration

To change the Kibana configuration, follow these steps:

1. Run the following command in the terminal to open the configuration file:

   ```
   sudo vi ~/kibana-4.1.1-linux-x64/config/kibana.yml
   ```

   Windows users can open the `kibana.yml` file from the `config` folder.

In this file, you can change various parameters such as the port on which Kibana works, the host address on which Kibana works, the URL of Elasticsearch that you wish to connect to, and so on.

2. For example, the port on which Kibana works can be changed by changing the port address. As shown in the following screenshot, `port: 5601` can be changed to any other port, such as `port: 5604`. Then we save the file.

```
 Kibana is served by a back end server. This controls which port to use.
port: 5604

# The host to bind the server to.
host: "0.0.0.0"

# The Elasticsearch instance to use for all your queries.
elasticsearch_url: "http://localhost:9200"

# preserve_elasticsearch_host true will send the hostname specified in 'elasticsearch'. If you set it to false,
# then the host you use to connect to *this* Kibana instance will be sent.
elasticsearch_preserve_host: true

# Kibana uses an index in Elasticsearch to store saved searches, visualizations
# and dashboards. It will create a new index if it doesn't already exist.
kibana_index: ".kibana"

# If your Elasticsearch is protected with basic auth, this is the user credentials
# used by the Kibana server to perform maintence on the kibana_index at statup. Your Kibana
# users will still need to authenticate with Elasticsearch (which is proxied thorugh
# the Kibana server)
# kibana_elasticsearch_username: user
# kibana_elasticsearch_password: pass

# If your Elasticsearch requires client certificate and key
# kibana_elasticsearch_client_crt: /path/to/your/client.crt
# kibana_elasticsearch_client_key: /path/to/your/client.key

# If you need to provide a CA certificate for your Elasticsarech instance, put
# the path of the pem file here.
# ca: /path/to/your/CA.pem

# The default application to load.
default_app_id: "discover"

# Time in milliseconds to wait for responses from the back end or elasticsearch.
# This must be > 0
request_timeout: 300000

# Time in milliseconds for Elasticsearch to wait for responses from shards.
"~/kibana-4.0.2-linux-x64/config/kibana.yml" 66 lines, 2355 characters
```

3. To check whether Kibana is running on port `5604`, run Kibana as mentioned earlier. Then open `http://localhost:5604` in the browser to verify, as follows:

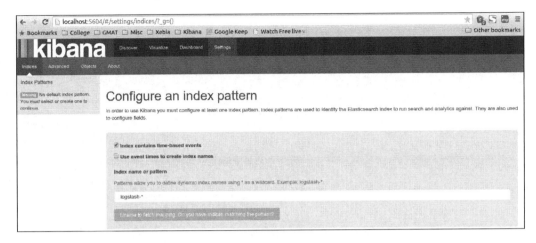

In the preceding screenshot, notice that Kibana is working on port `5604`, as per our change.

Importing a JSON file into Elasticsearch

To import a JSON file into Elasticsearch, we will use the `elasticdump` package. It is a set of import and export tools used for Elasticsearch. It makes it easier to copy, move, and save indexes. To install `elasticdump`, we will require npm and Node.js as prerequisites.

Installation of npm

In this section, npm along with Node.js will be installed. This section covers the installation of npm and Node.js on Ubuntu and Windows separately.

Installation of npm on Ubuntu 14.04

To install npm on Ubuntu, perform the following steps:

1. Add the official Node.js PPA:

```
sudo curl --silent --location  https://deb.nodesource.com/
setup_0.12 | sudo bash -
```

```
yuvraj@L212:~$ curl --silent --location https://deb.nodesource.com/setup_0.12 | sudo bash -

## Installing the NodeSource Node.js 0.12 repo...


## Populating apt-get cache...

+ apt-get update
Ign http://dl.google.com stable InRelease
Hit http://dl.google.com stable Release.gpg
Hit http://dl.google.com stable Release
Hit http://dl.google.com stable/main amd64 Packages
Hit http://dl.google.com stable/main i386 Packages
Ign http://extras.ubuntu.com trusty InRelease
Ign http://security.ubuntu.com trusty-security InRelease
Ign http://archive.canonical.com trusty InRelease
Hit http://security.ubuntu.com trusty-security Release.gpg
Hit http://archive.canonical.com trusty Release.gpg
Hit http://security.ubuntu.com trusty-security Release
Hit http://archive.canonical.com trusty Release
Ign http://dl.google.com stable/main Translation-en_IN
Ign http://dl.google.com stable/main Translation-en
Hit http://security.ubuntu.com trusty-security/main Sources
Hit http://security.ubuntu.com trusty-security/restricted Sources
Hit http://security.ubuntu.com trusty-security/universe Sources
```

As shown in the preceding screenshot, the command will add the official Node.js repository to the system and update the apt package database to include all the latest files under the packages. At the end of the execution of this command, we will be prompted to install Node.js and npm, as shown in the following screenshot:

```
Hit http://in.archive.ubuntu.com trusty-backports/multiverse i386 Packages
Hit http://in.archive.ubuntu.com trusty-backports/main Translation-en
Hit http://in.archive.ubuntu.com trusty-backports/multiverse Translation-en
Hit http://in.archive.ubuntu.com trusty-backports/restricted Translation-en
Hit http://in.archive.ubuntu.com trusty-backports/universe Translation-en
Ign http://in.archive.ubuntu.com trusty/main Translation-en_IN
Ign http://in.archive.ubuntu.com trusty/multiverse Translation-en_IN
Ign http://in.archive.ubuntu.com trusty/restricted Translation-en_IN
Ign http://in.archive.ubuntu.com trusty/universe Translation-en_IN
Fetched 6,627 B in 31s (210 B/s)
Reading package lists... Done

## Run `apt-get install nodejs` (as root) to install Node.js 0.12 and npm
```

2. Install Node.js by entering this command in the terminal:

```
sudo apt-get install --yes nodejs
```

```
yuvraj@L212:~$ sudo apt-get install --yes nodejs
Reading package lists... Done
Building dependency tree
Reading state information... Done
The following packages were automatically installed and are no longer required:
  gyp libamd2.3.1 libbabl-0.1-0 libc-ares-dev libc-ares2 libcamd2.3.1
  libccolamd2.8.0 libcholmod2.1.2 libgegl-0.2-0 libgfortran3
  libjavascriptcoregtk-1.0-0 libjs-node-uuid liblapack3 libmng2 libssl-dev
  libssl-doc libumfpack5.6.2 libunibreak1 libv8-3.14-dev libv8-3.14.5
  libwebkitgtk-1.0-0 libwebkitgtk-1.0-common libzlcore-data libzlcore0.12
  libzltext-data libzltext0.12 libzlui-qt4 zlib1g-dev
Use 'apt-get autoremove' to remove them.
The following NEW packages will be installed:
  nodejs
0 upgraded, 1 newly installed, 0 to remove and 107 not upgraded.
Need to get 5,416 kB of archives.
After this operation, 26.8 MB of additional disk space will be used.
Get:1 https://deb.nodesource.com/node_0.12/ trusty/main nodejs amd64 0.12.7-1nodesource1~trusty1 [5,416 kB]
Fetched 5,416 kB in 10min 16s (8,780 B/s)
Selecting previously unselected package nodejs.
(Reading database ... 225502 files and directories currently installed.)
Preparing to unpack .../nodejs_0.12.7-1nodesource1~trusty1_amd64.deb ...
Unpacking nodejs (0.12.7-1nodesource1~trusty1) ...
Processing triggers for man-db (2.6.7.1-1ubuntu1) ...
Setting up nodejs (0.12.7-1nodesource1~trusty1) ...
```

 This will automatically install Node.js and npm as npm is bundled within Node.js.

3. To check whether Node.js has been installed successfully, type the following command in the terminal:

```
node -v
```

Upon successful installation, it will display the version of Node.js.

4. Now, to check whether npm has been installed successfully, type the following command in the terminal:

```
npm -v
```

Upon successful installation, it will show the version of npm.

Installation of npm on Windows

To install npm on Windows, follow these steps:

1. Download the Windows Installer (.msi) file by going to https://nodejs.org/en/download/.

2. Double-click on the downloaded file and keep clicking on **Next** to install the software.

3. To validate the successful installation of Node.js, right-click and select **GIT Bash**.

   In GIT Bash, enter this:

   ```
   node -v
   ```

   Upon successful installation, you will be shown the version of Node.js.

4. To validate the successful installation of npm, right-click and select **GIT Bash**.

   In GIT Bash, enter the following line:

   ```
   npm -v
   ```

   Upon successful installation, it will show the version of npm.

Installing elasticdump

In this section, elasticdump will be installed. It will be used to import a JSON file into Elasticsearch. It requires npm and Node.js installed. This section covers the installation on Ubuntu and Windows separately.

Installing elasticdump on Ubuntu 14.04

Perform these steps to install elasticdump on Ubuntu:

1. Install elasticdump by typing the following command in the terminal:

   ```
   sudo npm install elasticdump -g
   ```

2. Then run elasticdump by typing this command in the terminal:

   ```
   elasticdump
   ```

3. Import a sample data (JSON) file into Elasticsearch, which can be downloaded from https://github.com/guptayuvraj/Kibana_Essentials and is named tweet.json. It will be imported into Elasticsearch using the following command in the terminal:

   ```
   elasticdump \
   --bulk=true \
   ```

```
--input="/home/yuvraj/Desktop/tweet.json" \
--output=http://localhost:9200/
```

Here, `input` provides the location of the file, as shown in the following screenshot:

```
yuvraj@L212:~$ elasticdump \
> --bulk=true \
> --input="/home/yuvraj/Desktop/tweet.json" \
> --output=http://localhost:9200/
Wed, 01 Jul 2015 10:24:44 GMT | starting dump
Wed, 01 Jul 2015 10:24:44 GMT | got 100 objects from source file (offset: 0)
Wed, 01 Jul 2015 10:24:46 GMT | sent 100 objects to destination elasticsearch, wrote 100
Wed, 01 Jul 2015 10:24:46 GMT | got 100 objects from source file (offset: 100)
Wed, 01 Jul 2015 10:24:46 GMT | sent 100 objects to destination elasticsearch, wrote 100
Wed, 01 Jul 2015 10:24:46 GMT | got 100 objects from source file (offset: 200)
Wed, 01 Jul 2015 10:24:46 GMT | sent 100 objects to destination elasticsearch, wrote 100
Wed, 01 Jul 2015 10:24:46 GMT | got 100 objects from source file (offset: 300)
Wed, 01 Jul 2015 10:24:47 GMT | sent 100 objects to destination elasticsearch, wrote 100
Wed, 01 Jul 2015 10:24:47 GMT | got 100 objects from source file (offset: 400)
Wed, 01 Jul 2015 10:24:47 GMT | sent 100 objects to destination elasticsearch, wrote 100
Wed, 01 Jul 2015 10:24:47 GMT | got 100 objects from source file (offset: 500)
Wed, 01 Jul 2015 10:24:47 GMT | sent 100 objects to destination elasticsearch, wrote 100
Wed, 01 Jul 2015 10:24:47 GMT | got 100 objects from source file (offset: 600)
Wed, 01 Jul 2015 10:24:47 GMT | sent 100 objects to destination elasticsearch, wrote 100
Wed, 01 Jul 2015 10:24:47 GMT | got 100 objects from source file (offset: 700)
Wed, 01 Jul 2015 10:24:47 GMT | sent 100 objects to destination elasticsearch, wrote 100
Wed, 01 Jul 2015 10:24:47 GMT | got 100 objects from source file (offset: 800)
Wed, 01 Jul 2015 10:24:48 GMT | sent 100 objects to destination elasticsearch, wrote 100
```

As you can see, data is being imported to Elasticsearch from the `tweet.json` file, and the dump complete message is displayed when all the records are imported to Elasticsearch successfully.

 Elasticsearch should be running while importing the sample file.

Installing elasticdump on Windows

To install `elasticdump` on Windows, perform the following steps:

1. Install `elasticdump` by typing the following command in **GIT Bash**:

   ```
   npm install elasticdump -g
   ```

```
ygupta@XE-T-YGUPTA ~/Desktop/Personal/Kibana/elasticsearch-1.5.2
$ npm install elasticdump -g
C:\Users\ygupta\AppData\Roaming\npm\multielasticdump -> C:\Users\ygupta\AppData\
Roaming\npm\node_modules\elasticdump\bin\multielasticdump
C:\Users\ygupta\AppData\Roaming\npm\elasticdump -> C:\Users\ygupta\AppData\Roami
ng\npm\node_modules\elasticdump\bin\elasticdump
elasticdump@0.14.1 C:\Users\ygupta\AppData\Roaming\npm\node_modules\elasticdump
├── line-reader@0.2.4
├── optimist@0.6.1 (wordwrap@0.0.3, minimist@0.0.10)
├── JSONStream@0.9.0 (through@2.3.7, jsonparse@0.0.5)
├── request@2.58.0 (caseless@0.10.0, forever-agent@0.6.1, aws-sign2@0.5.0, strin
gstream@0.0.4, tunnel-agent@0.4.0, oauth-sign@0.8.0, isstream@0.1.2, extend@2.0.
1, json-stringify-safe@5.0.1, node-uuid@1.4.3, qs@3.1.0, combined-stream@1.0.5,
mime-types@2.0.14, tough-cookie@2.0.0, http-signature@0.11.0, bl@0.9.4, hawk@2.3
.1, form-data@1.0.0-rc1, har-validator@1.8.0)
```

2. Then run `elasticdump` by typing this command in **GIT Bash**:

   `elasticdump`

3. Import the sample data (JSON) file into Elasticsearch, which can be downloaded from `https://github.com/guptayuvraj/Kibana_Essentials` and is named `tweet.json`. It will be imported to Elasticsearch using the following command in **GIT Bash**:

   `elasticdump \`

   `--bulk=true \`

   `--input="C:\Users\ygupta\Desktop\tweet.json" \`

   `--output=http://localhost:9200/`

   Here, `input` provides the location of the file.

```
MINGW32:/C/Users/ygupta/Desktop
ygupta@XE-T-YGUPTA /C/Users/ygupta/Desktop
$ elasticdump \
> --bulk=true \
> --input="C:\Users\ygupta\Desktop\tweet.json" \
> --output=http://localhost:9200/
Sat, 27 Jun 2015 10:08:25 GMT | starting dump
Sat, 27 Jun 2015 10:08:25 GMT | got 100 objects from source file (offset: 0)
Sat, 27 Jun 2015 10:08:25 GMT | sent 100 objects to destination elasticsearch, w
rote 100
Sat, 27 Jun 2015 10:08:25 GMT | got 100 objects from source file (offset: 100)
Sat, 27 Jun 2015 10:08:26 GMT | sent 100 objects to destination elasticsearch, w
rote 100
Sat, 27 Jun 2015 10:08:26 GMT | got 100 objects from source file (offset: 200)
Sat, 27 Jun 2015 10:08:26 GMT | sent 100 objects to destination elasticsearch, w
rote 100
Sat, 27 Jun 2015 10:08:26 GMT | got 100 objects from source file (offset: 300)
Sat, 27 Jun 2015 10:08:26 GMT | sent 100 objects to destination elasticsearch, w
rote 100
Sat, 27 Jun 2015 10:08:26 GMT | got 100 objects from source file (offset: 400)
Sat, 27 Jun 2015 10:08:26 GMT | sent 100 objects to destination elasticsearch, w
rote 100
Sat, 27 Jun 2015 10:08:26 GMT | got 100 objects from source file (offset: 500)
Sat, 27 Jun 2015 10:08:26 GMT | sent 100 objects to destination elasticsearch, w
rote 100
Sat, 27 Jun 2015 10:08:26 GMT | got 100 objects from source file (offset: 600)
```

The preceding screenshot shows data being imported to Elasticsearch from the `tweet.json` file, and the dump complete message is displayed when all the records are imported to Elasticsearch successfully.

 Elasticsearch should be running while importing the sample file.

To verify that the data has been imported to Elasticsearch, open `http://localhost:5601` in your browser, and this is what you should see:

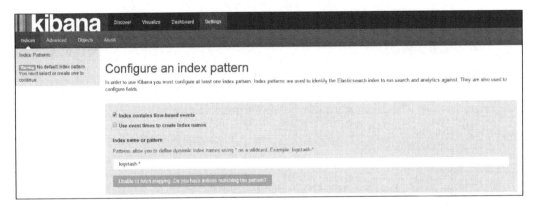

When Kibana is opened, you have to configure an index pattern. So, if data has been imported, you can enter the index name, which is mentioned in the `tweet.json` file as `index: tweet`. After the page loads, you can see to the left under **Index Patterns** the name of the index that has been imported (`tweet`).

Now mention the index name as `tweet`. It will then automatically detect the timestamped field and will provide you with an option to select the field. If there are multiple fields, then you can select them by clicking on **Time-field name**, which will provide a drop-down list of all fields available, as shown here:

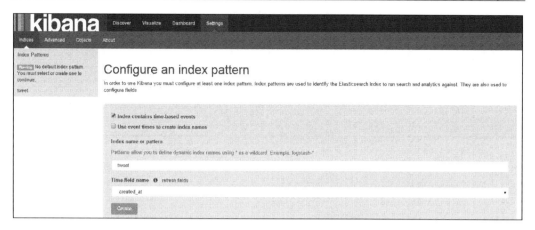

Finally, click on **Create** to create the index in Kibana. After you have clicked on
Create, it will display the various fields present in this index.

> If you do not get the options of **Time-field name** and **Create** after
> entering the index name as tweet, it means that the data has not
> been imported into Elasticsearch.

Summary

In this chapter, you learned about Kibana, along with the basic concepts of
Elasticsearch. These help in the easy understanding of Kibana. We also looked at
the prerequisites for installing Kibana, followed by a detailed explanation of how
to install each component individually in Ubuntu and Windows. By the end, you
learned how to import a sample JSON data file into Elasticsearch, which will be
beneficial in the upcoming chapters.

In the next chapter, you will understand the **Discover** tab in Kibana, along with the
working of each of its components. You will also learn how Kibana uses it for better
understanding of data.

2
Exploring the Discover Page

Discover is one of the pages present in Kibana 4 that helps you to play around with your data. The **Discover** page is very crucial and plays an important role in understanding what your data is, what your data means, and how you can use this data for different kinds of visualization. This page gives you a full overview of your data including listings of indexes, listings of fields, and showing text contained in fields. In this page, you can view all the data stored in different indexes by changing the index pattern. You can search for data, query data, filter data, and view search results. Every search query result shows the matching documents. You can also view field-specific data on this page. Histogram is displayed on this page, which helps you to view your data on a time basis for which a time field has to be specified for every index.

The **Discover** page contains the following notable components:

- Time filter
- Toolbar
- Index name
- Fields list
- Document data
- Histogram (on basis of time)
- Hits

In this chapter, we will go through all these components in brief.

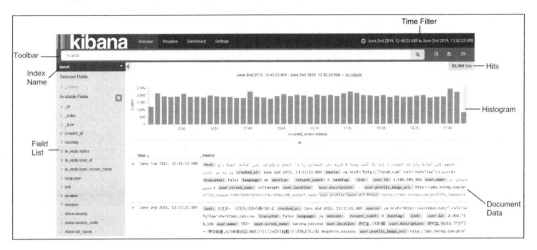

The previous figure contains the following:

- **Time filter**: This contains data of a particular time interval
- **Toolbar**: This consists of a search bar along with the option of new search, save search, load saved search, and settings
- **Index name**: This shows the name of the selected index
- **Fields list**: This contains all the fields within the selected index
- **Hits**: This contains the matching documents in the selected time interval
- **Histogram**: This shows the distribution of all the documents matching the time filter in the selected index
- **Document data**: This contains all the documents along with the data in the entire field as selected

Understanding the time filter

The time filter is a very powerful component that helps to drill down on data on a per time basis. It helps to see data of a specified time range. The time filter can be enabled/set only if the index contains a time field or time-based events. It eases the process of viewing large amounts of data but needing only to view data of a particular time, day, month, or year.

For example, if a news company is collecting Twitter tweets for its company hashtag but wants to analyze tweets tweeted between 8 p.m. and 9 p.m., then the time filter will be set to show data only between 8 p.m. and 9 p.m., which helps in easy analysis of data.

Time filter shows data of the last 15 minutes, as per the default settings. You can change the time range or select a specific time range by using **Time Picker**.

Before setting the time filter, let's examine the date and time interval for the tweets stored in the sample data of the `tweet.json` file. The tweets are stored in the UTC time zone and tweets are fetched between the time interval of 07:15:23 (UTC time) and 08:02:22 (UTC time) for June 2, 2015. Kibana recognizes the time interval as per the system time zone, therefore Kibana automatically converts the data timestamp from the UTC time zone to the system time zone for the sample data.

Let's learn more about various options for setting time filter using **Time Picker**.

Setting the time filter

Click on the time filter shown in the previous figure, which is in the top-right corner, to open the **Time Picker**.

Now we have three options for selecting a time filter: **Quick**, **Relative**, and **Absolute**:

- In the **Quick** time filter, select any one of the given fields (such as **Today**, **This year**, **Previous month**, **Last 15 minutes**, **Last 30 days**, and so on) to set the time filter:

In the previous figure, the various fields are provided within the **Quick** time filter to select and set a time range. It is a very quick way to automatically set a time filter as per the user's needs and requirements, just by clicking on a shortcut field.

- Click on **Relative** to define a relative time filter. In this time filter option, you can enter the relative starting time span you are looking for. You have the option of setting relative start times in terms of seconds, minutes, hours, days, weeks, months, and years:

In the previous figure, there is a textbox in which you can enter a numeric number and group it with the different options of seconds, minutes, hours, days, weeks, months or years, to set a relative time filter.

Also, there is a small checkbox that helps to round the time to the nearest seconds/minutes/hours/days/weeks/months or years as selected. If you tick the checkbox then it will automatically round the time as per your selected option.

For example, if you are viewing data of relative time 24 hours ago, and suppose that time is 11:45:56 (hours: minutes: seconds), if you tick the checkbox then your time will be rounded to the previous hour, namely 11:00:00 (hours: minutes: seconds).

If you are viewing data of relative time 400 minutes ago, and suppose that time is 06:25:34 (hours: minutes: seconds), if you tick the checkbox then your time will be rounded to the previous minute, namely 06:25:00 (hours: minutes: seconds):

We can also tick the checkbox beside the round to the minute box to round the time to the nearest unit as shown in the following figure:

- Click on **Absolute** to define an absolute time filter. In this time filter option, you can enter the starting date/time using the **From** field and enter the end date in the **To** field, specifying date/time in the format of `YYYY-MM-DD HH:mm:ss.SSS`:

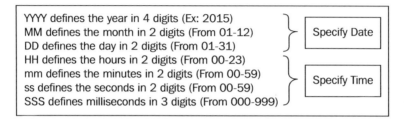

In the previous figure, the **From** field in which the date/time is specified, and the **To** field in which the date/time is specified, are shown. Whatever time is chosen, it will also be reflected in the time filter, which is in the top-right corner.

The time filter has to be specified for June 2 (as per the UTC time zone), which can be specified easily by using either the **Quick** time filter option or the **Absolute** time filter option.

You can also set the time filter from the histogram in the following ways:

- Click on any of the bars shown in the histogram to view data as per the time interval mentioned.

  For example, if the histogram is created in which each bar shows data of a minute, then by clicking on any of the bars you can get all the data of that particular minute, and the histogram will be redrawn to show distribution of data on a per second basis.

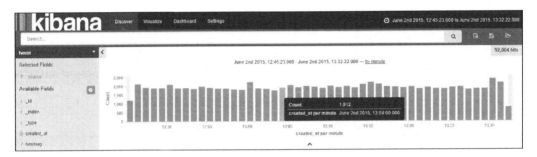

In the previous figure, the histogram is clicked at a particular minute, namely **13:04:00.000**, following the time format:

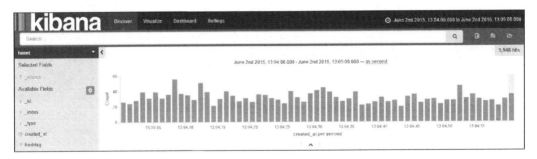

In the previous figure, we are getting data of only the minute that was selected, for example, **13:04:00.000**, which allows you to easily analyze data of a particular minute. Here, the histogram has been redrawn to show data distribution on a per second basis. You can also see in the time filter in the top-right corner, the time filter has changed for the particular minute that was selected.

 In this book, we are using the system time zone as IST. IST is 5 hr 30 min ahead of UTC, therefore the time for data stored is from **12:45:23.000** (hr, min, sec, ms) to **13:32:22.000** (hr, min, sec, ms).

- Click and drag the cursor to view a specific time range. This can be done easily by hovering the cursor anywhere over the bar chart, upon which the cursor reshapes to a plus (+) sign, which indicates the start point. After the cursor changes to a plus sign, click and drag the cursor to select a time range:

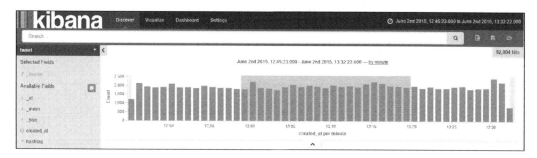

In the previous figure, the cursor was dragged to select a specific time interval:

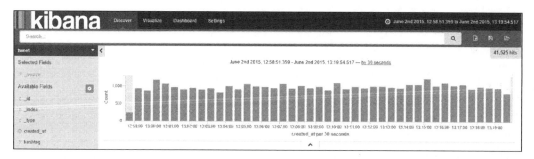

In the previous figure, the data in the document table is changed as per the time range interval specified. Here, the histogram has been redrawn to show data distribution on the basis of 30 seconds. Also, the time interval specified has been changed in the time filter, which is in the top-right corner.

In Kibana 4, you can undo any changes made by either clicking on the backspace button on the keyboard or back button of the browser. Also you can close/hide **Time Picker** by clicking on the caret (^), which is at the bottom of **Time Picker** or by clicking on the time filter component.

The Auto-refresh page

The refresh interval option is used to automatically refresh the **Discover** page with the streaming data flown in the index. It reloads the page with the latest data by resubmitting the query of loading data. It provides different options for specifying refresh intervals such as 5 seconds, 15 minutes, 2 hours, 1 day, and so on.

The various options provided in the refresh interval are shown in the previous figure.

To set a refresh interval, perform the following steps:

1. Click on the time filter, which is at the top-right corner of the page.
2. Click on the **Auto-refresh** option, which is in the main menu to the left-hand corner of the time filter.
3. Choose any of the options provided by the refresh interval tab.

Whenever the refresh interval is chosen, the refresh interval option appears to the left-hand side of the time filter in the main menu bar, which is shown in the following figure:

The refresh interval option is very useful when you have continuous streaming of data into Elasticsearch and want to analyze the data on the fly.

Understanding the toolbar

The toolbar is one of the most crucial components of the **Discover** page, which helps with powerful analysis of data based on search queries and filters as applied. It is used for specifying the search query that is used for analyzing the data. Whenever a search query is specified, it checks in all documents and returns results of the matching search query. The toolbar consists of a search bar along with option buttons such as new search, save search, and load saved search.

Let's understand the usage of different options of the toolbar in detail.

Using the search bar

The search bar is used to search for a particular word, for example, a term either contained in all the documents or for searching for a particular term in a specific field in all the documents. Whenever a search query is submitted, it matches the documents of the selected index and returns the results. For searching a query, you can specify basic simple strings or use Apache Lucene query syntax. As Kibana leverages the functionality of Elasticsearch, Lucene query provides a way to use simple and complex queries, providing powerful search capabilities for playing with data.

Whenever a search query is submitted, corresponding hits, histogram, document data, and fields get updated as per the search results obtained. Hits indicate the total number of documents matching the search results. It is displayed in the top-right corner, just above the histogram. Document data displays the initial 500 documents as per the default settings. Also, the search results are highlighted in Kibana 4, which provides an elegant way to view the search result.

The different ways of searching data are as follows:

- To search data (term) that is contained in any field in all the documents, just type the data that you would like to search.

  For example, if you want to search for Windows, enter `windows` to search within all fields in all documents:

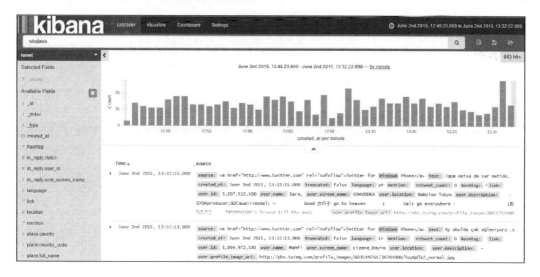

In the previous figure, **Windows** was searched for and was found in 643 documents as specified by 643 hits. In this example, it will search within all the fields contained in the document and give corresponding results. As per the search results, hits, histogram, document data, and fields get updated.

- To search for data (term) in a specific field, you have to specify the field name followed by a colon, followed by the search term.

  For example, if you want to search for Windows in the text field, enter `text:windows`, which would provide you with all the documents matching the term **windows** in the text field:

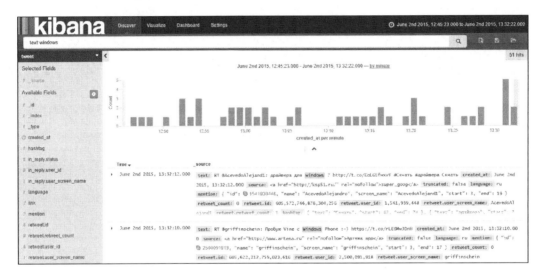

In the previous figure, searching for `windows` in the text field provided 51 matching documents. In this example it searched only within the text field of all the documents. As per the search results, hits, histogram, document data and fields get updated.

- To search for an exact data phrase (a string containing multiple words), enclose the data within double quotes (" "). It will search for exactly that data phrase within all the documents.

For example, if you want to search for Windows 10, enter `"windows 10"`, which would provide you with all the documents matching the term **windows 10** in the documents:

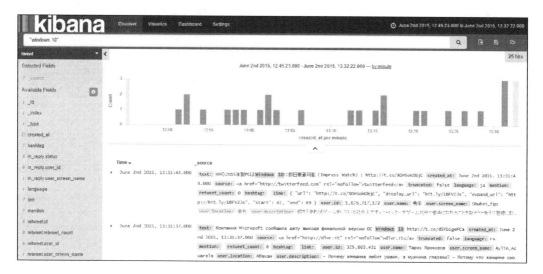

In the previous figure, searching for `"windows 10"` provided 25 hits (matching documents). In this example, it searched for documents containing the exact phrase **windows 10**, which were displayed in the search results.

 Searching for phrases using double quotes can be done similarly for searching in a specific field.

- To search data for a particular range, you can specify it using the brackets (`[]`) containing a starting value to ending value as [starting value TO ending value]. In the range, the data can be specified as multiple data types such as date, integer, or string.

For example, if you want to search data within a specified date range, just enter the date field name followed by the date range. Enter `created_at:[2015-06-02 TO 2015-06-03]` in the search bar, which would provide you with all the documents occurring in the specified date range. The date format is being followed as per the Elasticsearch format, which was mentioned earlier in this chapter while explaining the **Absolute** time filter:

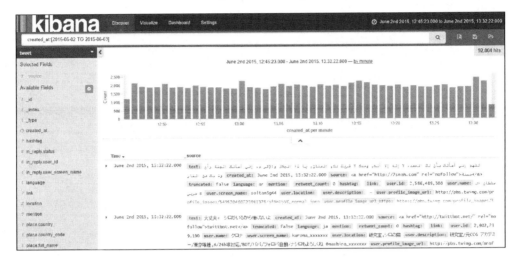

In the previous figure, searching for a date range provided all the documents occurring in the specified date range.

- To search data for a particular range containing string values, it will follow the same syntax of range as specified previously.

For example, if you want to search data for a range of string, enter `text:[ubuntu TO windows]` and it will provide search results containing words lying between Ubuntu and Windows in the text field:

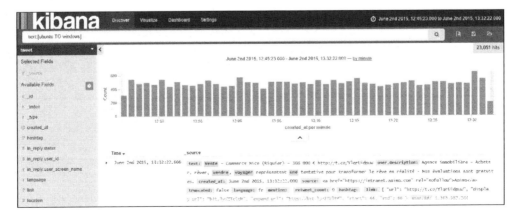

In the previous figure, the search results highlighted all the matching documents containing words between Ubuntu and Windows following alphabetical order. **Vente, vendre,** and **voyager** all lie between the words Ubuntu and Windows.

 The TO keyword has to be specified in capital letters otherwise the search will not give any results and show it as an error in query syntax. Warning: the TO keyword is very inefficient to use.

- To search for more complex queries, make use of Boolean operators that consist of OR, AND, NOT, +, or -. All the Boolean operators have to be specified in capital letters otherwise it will treat it as a simple word:

  ○ The OR operator is used to combine multiple words and if either of the words is found in any of the documents, it will show the matching documents. Its analogy is similar to union in sets. To use this operator we can specify OR or || (double pipe) symbol.

  For example, if you want to search for Windows or Mac within all documents, enter windows OR mac, which would provide all the matching documents containing either the terms **Windows** or **Mac**:

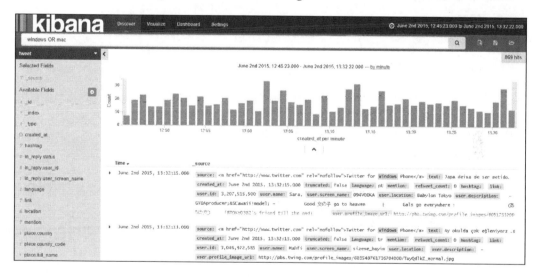

In the previous figure, the search results highlighted all the documents containing either the terms **Windows** or **Mac**.

> The OR operator is the default operator when searching between two or more terms if no operator is specified. So, if you specify `windows 10` (without double quotes) it will give you matching documents containing either the **windows** word or **10** as an integer value.

○ The AND operator is used to combine multiple words and if both of the words exist in any document, it will show the matching documents. Its analogy is similar to intersections in sets. To use this operator we can specify AND or && (double ampersand) symbol.

For example, if you want to search for Windows and Mac within all documents, enter `windows AND mac`, which would provide all the matching documents containing the terms **Windows** and **Mac**:

In the previous figure, the search results highlighted all the documents containing both the terms **Windows** and **Mac**.

○ The NOT operator is used for excluding searching in documents containing any term occurring after the NOT operator. Its analogy is similar to difference in sets. To use this operator we can specify the NOT (exclamation) symbol.

For example, if you want to search for Windows but not for Mac within all documents, enter `windows NOT mac`, which would provide all the matching documents containing the term **Windows** but not the term **Mac**:

In the previous figure, the search results highlighted all the documents containing the word **Windows** but not the word **Mac**.

○ The + operator is also known as a required operator. It is used to include words that must exist in any document occurring after the + operator. This operator is similar to combining NOT along with the AND operator.

For example, if you want to search for Windows and maybe Mac within all documents, enter +windows mac, which would provide all the matching documents containing the word **Windows** and may contain the word **Mac**.

In the previous figure, the matching document is equal to 643 hits, meaning an equivalent of 642 hits (windows NOT mac) and 1 hit (windows AND mac).

In the previous figure, the search results highlighted all the documents that must have the word **Windows** and may or may not contain the word **Mac**.

○ The - operator is also known as the prohibit operator. It is used for excluding searching in documents containing any word occurring after the - operator. This operator is similar to the NOT operator.

For example, if you want to search for Windows but not for Mac within all documents, enter `"windows"-"mac"`, which would provide all the matching documents containing the term **Windows** and not the term **Mac**:

In the previous figure, the search results highlighted all the documents containing the word **Windows** but not the word **Mac**.

- Grouping is used for performing more complex queries by combining multiple Boolean operators. It uses parenthesis () for grouping Boolean operators.

For example, if you want to search for either **Mac** or **Linux** and **Windows**, enter (mac OR linux) AND windows. To simplify, all the documents must have the term **Windows** and contain either the terms **Mac** or **Linux**. It is similar to combining (mac AND windows) along with (linux AND windows):

In the previous figure, the search results highlighted all the documents containing the term **Windows** with a combination of either **Linux** or **Mac**.

- Wildcard searches are supported by Apache Lucene, which is the underlying layer of Kibana that is abstracted by Elasticsearch. It provides single character and multiple character searches. The single character searches are done using the ? (question mark) symbol whereas multiple character searches are done using the * (asterisk) symbol. For a single character wildcard search, it looks for terms that match with the single character that has to be replaced.

  For example, if you want to search for terms, such as mac or sac or pac, enter the search as ?ac. It will match all the documents to give results matching this wildcard expression. It would be any initial letter followed by **ac** and would consist of three characters only:

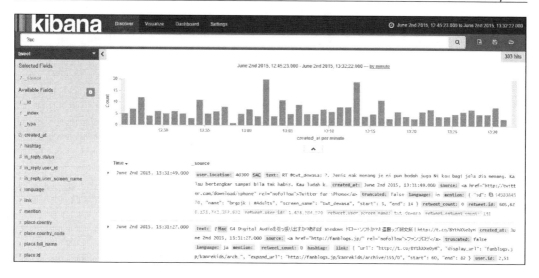

In the previous figure, the search results highlighted all the documents matching the wildcard expression ?ac, matching with words such as **sac**, **mac**, and **tac**.

For a multiple characters wildcard search, it looks for terms that match 0 or more than 0 characters.

For example, if you want to search for terms such as Mac, Macintosh, machine, and so on, enter the search as mac*. It will match all documents to give results matching this wildcard expression. It would contain results following a pattern starting with **mac** and followed by 0 or more characters:

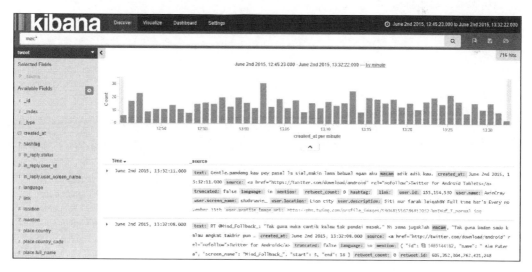

In the previous figure, the search results highlighted all the documents matching the wildcard expression `mac*`, matching with words such as **macht**, **mac**, **macam**, and so on.

> Wildcard searches are not applicable for multiple words/phrases and are only applicable on a single word/term. Wildcard searches work even in the middle of the terms such as `m?c`, matching words like **mac**, **mic**, **mgc**, and so on, and `m*c` matching words like **mac**, **music**, **mufc**, and so on.

- Proximity searches are used to find terms that are within a definite distance apart from each other, for example to match documents containing two terms that are at a definite distance apart from each other. It uses the ~ (tilde) symbol for performing a proximity search, which appears at the end of a phrase/multiple words.

For example, if you want to search for documents containing the terms Linux and Mac within seven words of each other, enter `"linux mac"~7`. It will match all documents to show results of documents containing both terms within a distance of seven words:

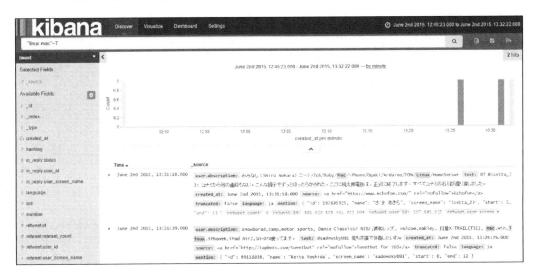

In the previous figure, the search results highlighted all the documents matching a proximity search of having both terms **linux** and **mac** appear within seven words of each other.

In a proximity search, changing the position of terms doesn't make any difference. Therefore searching `"linux mac"~7` or `"mac linux"~7` will show the same results.

- Regular expressions are used to find terms that follow a specified pattern. It can be used on words, phrases, or specific fields. It helps to form complex queries allowing it to be used with multiple words as well. It overcomes the limitation of a wildcard search and allows it to be used even with phrases. It uses / (slash) along with [] (square brackets) in which different characters are specified to search for a given pattern.

  For example, if you want to search for phrases containing words such as mac, mat, mag, combined with words such as it, in, enter `/ma[ctg]/ AND /i[tn]/`. It will match all documents containing both sets of words:

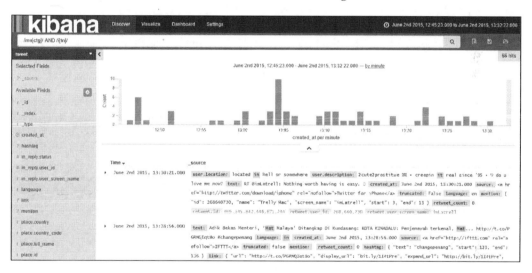

In the previous figure, the search results highlighted all the documents containing words like **mac**, **mat** combined with **it** and **in**.

 Regular expressions are very inefficient for searching.

New Search

New Search provides the option to start a new search. It erases the present search query and creates a new search to play around with data. It is done by clicking on the **New Search** button ▣, which is situated in the toolbar beside the search bar:

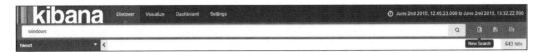

In the previous figure, notice the New Search option, which is accessible from the toolbar.

Save Search

Save Search provides the option of saving a search query. It is used to save the current entered search query along with the selected index information. This option is situated beside the New Search button in the toolbar.

To save a search, perform the following steps:

1. Enter the search query string in the search bar.
2. Click on the Save Search button 💾 present in the toolbar next to the New Search button:

3. Give this search a name to save. We will give `Search_Twitter` as the search name to save containing a search query of windows:

4. Click on **Save** to save the search.

You can close/hide the Save Search option by clicking on the caret (^), which is at the bottom of the Save Search area or by clicking on the Save Search button.

Load Saved Search

Load Saved Search provides the option of loading the saved search query. It is used to load a saved search with a specified index. If loading a saved search included a different index, then on loading it the selected index also gets updated. This option is situated beside the Save Search button in the toolbar.

To load a saved search, perform the following steps:

1. Click on the Load Saved Search button  present in the toolbar next to the Save Search button:

2. Specify the saved search name to load it. All the saved search queries are displayed below the search bar:

3. Click on it to load the saved search.

 You can close/hide the Load Saved Search option by clicking on the caret (^), which is at the bottom of the Load Saved Search area or by clicking on the Load Saved Search button.

Understanding the Fields list

The **Fields** list contains a listing of all the fields contained in the documents that appear within a selected index. The **Fields** list appears just beneath the index name on the left-hand side of the **Discover** page. It is used for knowing which fields appear in the data on the basis of which analysis can be done. It contains popular fields, selected fields, and all the other types of fields. Fields are displayed under each category in alphabetical order.

View field data information

This serves as an important metric that displays how many documents in the selected index will contain a specific field, what will be the top five values for the field, and the percentage breakdown of total documents containing the value.

 By default, document data contains 500 documents matching the search query as listed, although it can be modified by changing the **discover:sampleSize** option in advanced settings, which will be covered in *Chapter 5, Exploring the Settings Page*.

To see field data information, click on the name of the field in the **Fields** list. The field could be under any category, for example selected fields, popular fields, or other fields:

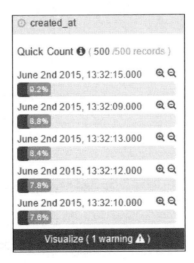

In the previous figure, by clicking on the **created_at** field, it is showing the top five values of the field, how many values of each specific field record exist in the current index, and the percentage breakdown of the fields in terms of total documents.

 The **Visualize** option provided is used to create a visualization based on a specific field by clicking the **Visualize** button beneath the field data information as shown in the previous figure.

Filtering by field

Filtering by field provides the flexibility of filtering the search results based on fields. Filter the search results in order to display documents matching the filter criterion. Filters can be added from the **Fields** list or document data.

There are two types of filters:

- **Positive filter**: This is denoted by a + (plus) symbol magnifier ⊕. It is used to display only those documents that contain the specific value for which it is being filtered.

- **Negative filter**: This is denoted by a - (minus) symbol magnifier ⊖. It is used to exclude all the documents containing that value in the specified field.

To add a filter using the **Fields** list, click on the field on the basis of which you want to Filter. Upon clicking the field it will show the top five field values, which were described previously in viewing field data information. To the right of the field values, there are two buttons corresponding to the positive filter and the negative filter:

- For adding a positive filter, click on the + (plus) symbol magnifier. For example, you need to find only those documents that contain India within the **place.country** field, then you would click on the **place.country** field and click on the positive filter symbol beside India. It will filter results based on matching the word India in the **place.country** field within all documents:

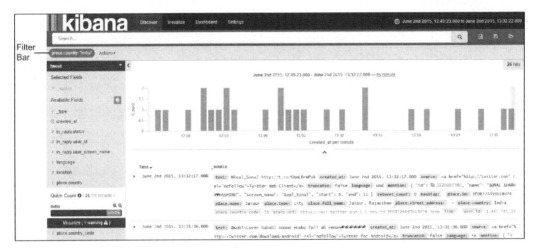

In the previous figure, the filter results show all the documents containing **India** within the **place.country** field. It also denotes 26 hits, meaning 26 matching documents containing **India** within the **place.country** field.

- To add a negative filter, click on the - (minus) symbol magnifier. For example, you need to find only those documents that do not contain **India** within the **place.country** field, then you would click on the **place. country** field and click on the negative filter symbol beside **India**. It will exclude all the documents matching India in the **place.country** field and show the remaining documents as a filtered result:

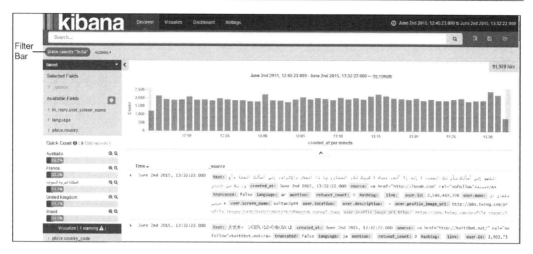

In the previous figure, the filter results show all the documents that do not contain **India** within the **place.country** field. It also denotes 91,978 hits, namely (92,004-26), which show all the matching documents that do not contain **India** within the **place.country** field.

> Whenever a filter is added, it shows below the search bar in the filter bar as shown in the previous figure.

To add a filter using document data, initially expand a document within the document data table by clicking on the expand button characterized by the ▶ symbol, which is found in the extreme left at the start of a document, beside the document's first column (generally it is **Time**). After clicking the expand button beside every field value on the left and beside every field name on the right, there are two buttons corresponding to the positive filter and the negative filter as per their convention:

- To add a positive filter, click on the + (plus) symbol magnifier ⊕

- To add a Negative Filter, click on the - (minus) symbol magnifier

In the previous figure, you can see the filter options available in document data through which you can apply a positive filter or a negative filter to a specified field.

 There will not be any filtering options provided in the fields that are not indexed in all the documents. To find the fields that are not indexes, using indices we can see information in advanced settings, which will be covered in *Chapter 5, Exploring the Settings Page*.

Functionalities of filters

After adding a filter, there are additional functionalities of filters that can be used to play around with filters easily. To view additional functionalities, click on the Actions link beside the added filter beneath the search bar, or hover over the filter added:

The Enable filter

This is used to enable the filter. After enabling the filter it will show the result that matches the filter only. Enabled filters are displayed in green. It is similar to a positive filter.

The Disable filter

This is used to disable the filter. Disabled filters are displayed in a striped shaded color:

The Pin filter

This is a newly added functionality in Kibana. It is used to pin a filter. After pinning a filter, it will persist across various Kibana pages. If you pin the filter in the **Discover** page then even if you move to the **Visualize** page or **Dashboard** page, the filter would be there. It is very useful as it reduces the effort of adding filters in different pages.

The Unpin filter

This is used to unpin the pinned filters.

The Invert filter

This is used to invert the filter. After inverting the filter, it will show the results that do not match the filter. After enabling the filter, it shows 91,978 results (92004-26). Inverted Filters are displayed in red. It is similar to a negative filter:

The Toggle filter

This is used to toggle the filter. Upon clicking the Toggle filter, it changes from enabled filter to disabled filter and vice versa. If the filter is enabled, it will change it to disabled. If the filter is disabled, it will change it to enabled.

The Remove filter

This is used to remove the added filters.

 For multiple filters added, you can change the functionalities of every individual filter added, providing you with some more customization options.

Understanding document data

Document data displays all the documents in the selected index. By default, document data shows 500 documents listed, with the most recent documents shown first. By default, document data displays the localized version of the specified time field in the selected index and document of field _source. In document data you can add field columns, remove field columns, view document data, and sort documents.

Add a field to document data

It is very simple to add a field to document data. Fields can be added from the **Fields** list, which is at the left side of the **Discover** page and below the index name.

To add a field to document data:

1. Hover your mouse over any field from the **Fields** list and click on the **Add** button as shown:

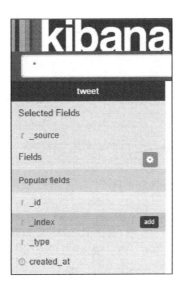

2. Repeat the previous step until all fields that you want to be displayed have been added to the document data.

For example, you want to add fields such as **_index, user.name, user.screen_ name, language**, then by adding such fields document data would display all the documents on the basis of these fields only.

In the previous figure, you can see all the document data containing the selected fields.

After adding fields to document data, the _source field is replaced in the **Fields** list and all the added fields appear within the selected fields category, which is displayed beneath the index name.

Remove a field from document data

It is very simple to remove a field from document data. Fields can be removed from the selected **Fields** list, which is at the left-hand side of the **Discover** page and below the index name.

To remove a field from document data, perform the following steps:

1. Hover your mouse over any field that you want to remove from the selected **Fields** list and click on the **Remove** button as shown:

2. Repeat the previous step until all fields have been removed that you want to drop from document data.

View data

To view the data in document data, perform the following steps:

1. Click on the expand button option characterized by the ▶ symbol, which is found in the extreme left at the start of a document, beside the document's first column (generally, this is **Time**). Kibana reads the document stored in Elasticsearch and displays it in tabular format showing all the document's fields. In the table, each row contains the field name followed by two filter buttons (the positive filter and the negative filter) and the field value:

2. Kibana can also display the document with all the field names and values in JSON format (pretty-printed), which was the original input format to Elasticsearch. To view documents in JSON format, click on the **JSON** tab:

3. Kibana can also display document data in a separate page, which can be accessed by clicking on the hyperlink provided, mentioned as **Link**, followed by index name, type name, and _id name. The link is provided on the right-hand side of the **Table** tab and **JSON** tab:

4. After clicking on the link, you will be redirected to a new tab in which the document is displayed in both the **Table** format and the **JSON** format. Also you can then share the link (URL) or bookmark the link (URL) for directly accessing the particular document:

localhost:5601/#/doc/tweet/tweet/tweet?id=6056456193407959048&_g=()

In the previous figure, you will notice the URL follows a format that is defined by specifying the host name on which Kibana is running, followed by doc (indicating document), index name, type name, and the _id name for the particular document.

To collapse document data, click on the collapse button characterized by the ▾ symbol, which is found in the extreme left at the start of a document, beside the document's first column (generally, this is **Time**).

Sorting documents

The sorting of document data can be done using the values in the indexed field. If there is any time field configured for a particular index name then, by default, documents are listed in reverse chronological order, with the newest documents on the basis of time shown first. For sorting documents, fields have to be added first to document data, which has been explained earlier in this chapter.

To change the sorting order within document data after adding a field, choose the field on the basis of which you want to sort your data. Then click on that specific field. The fields on the basis of which you can sort have a small Sort button, which is to the immediate right of the field name. You can also reverse the sort order by clicking on the field name the second time:

 Sorting is not done on those fields that contain the same value for all documents, such as _index, and _type field, as they contain only a single value in index and type name.

Moving fields in document data

You can rearrange the fields displayed in document data after adding the fields.

To rearrange the fields in the table, hover your mouse over the field name that you want to move. Just to the right-hand side of the field name (beside the Sort button), there is the option to move a column either to the right-hand side (>>) or left-hand side (<<) wherever applicable. If there is a time field specified in the index, the time value does not have an option of moving as the field is, by default, added and is not the added field. The left-most field name (after the time field) can only be moved towards the right-hand side:

The right-most field name can only be moved towards the left-hand side:

All the fields between them can be moved either to the left side:

Alternatively, they can be moved to the right-hand side:

Summary

In this chapter, we covered the various components of the **Discover** page. It provided an insight into the importance of using the **Discover** page, along with a proper understanding of the different components present in the **Discover** page. Also, each component was explained with the usage of various options present in the components.

In the next chapter, we will understand the **Visualize** page in Kibana, along with usage of various visualizations provided by Kibana. We will explore how Kibana provides easy-to-create visualizations.

3
Exploring the Visualize Page

The **Visualize** page is the most important page in Kibana 4, which helps in visualizing the data that has been analyzed using the **Discover** page. This page helps in creating the different types of visualization required for the data present in Elasticsearch. It is a separate page in Kibana that helps with easy understanding and creating data visualizations. This page is most crucial from a business perspective, because by analyzing the data stored, visualizations provide a simple and easy way to understand data. Using it, you can create different types of data visualization, save the visualizations, or use them individually/combine different visualizations to form a dashboard. This page gives you a full overview of the different types of visualization provided, how to create a new visualization from a new search or saved search, and how to design visualizations as per requirements.

The Kibana **Visualize** page is where you can create, modify, and view your own custom visualizations. There are several different types of visualization, including **Vertical Bar Chart**, **Area Chart**, **Line Chart**, **Pie Chart**, **Tile Map** (for displaying data on a map), and **Data Table**. Visualizations can also be shared with other users who have access to your Kibana instance.

Visualizations are the core component that makes Kibana functionality rich and useful software. Visualizations utilize the underlying component of Elasticsearch for aggregating and visualizing data. For a better understanding, let's explore the basic usage of aggregations used in Elasticsearch.

In this chapter, we are going to have a look at the following topics:

- Basic concepts of bucket aggregations
- Basic concepts of metric aggregations
- Steps for designing visualization
- Creating various visualizations

Understanding aggregations

Aggregations are collections of data that is stored in buckets. Aggregations have grown from the facets module of Elasticsearch, which allows fast querying and easy aggregation of data. Aggregations are used for building analytical information over the documents stored. They are used for real-time data analysis purposes. There are different types of aggregation which have a specified purpose with specific output, which can be classified into the following categories.

Bucket aggregations

In this type of aggregation, buckets are created to store various documents and are used for grouping the documents stored; every bucket is associated with a key and document criterion. The decision-making that decides which bucket will contain a document matching its criterion can be based either on the value of a specific field or any other parameter. Whenever aggregation is done, all bucket criterion are evaluated to decide which documents match the criterion of each bucket and fit into a particular bucket. This process goes on and on until all documents are segregated into different buckets as per the matching criterion. At the end of this process, all documents completely fit into any of the buckets created.

Every bucket has a criterion that helps to decide whether a document fits into that bucket or not. Also, bucket aggregations always compute and return the total number of documents that fit into each bucket. There are different bucket aggregators in Kibana 4 that have a different bucket strategy, such as some may define a single bucket, some may define multiple buckets, or dynamically create buckets during the aggregation process. Bucket aggregations are very powerful as they can combine with other types of aggregation, creating sub-aggregations. In sub-aggregations, the aggregations will be computed for each bucket generated by the parent aggregation. The different types of bucket aggregation are as follows.

Date histogram

This aggregation is done on date/time values that are automatically extracted by Kibana from the documents. Kibana automatically fetches the date type field in which different types of intervals are specified, such as 5 min, 30 min, and so on. This type of bucket puts in all the documents matching the criterion of the bucket whose value of the date field lies within the same interval as defined.

The available expressions for intervals specified in Kibana are year, quarter, month, week, day, hour, minute, second, auto, out of which only days, hours, minutes and seconds are allowed to contain fractional values. The auto interval automatically decides the time interval to be chosen by Kibana, on the basis of which graphs are designed, so that a good amount of buckets are created.

For example, date histogram can be used for a field that contains date/time with an interval of an hour. In this, there will be a bucket created for every hour, and each bucket stores documents that fall under the hour, meaning that if a document is created in the 5th hour, then the document fits into the bucket that contains documents created in the 5th hour only.

Histogram

This aggregation is done on a numeric field, which is automatically read/analyzed by Kibana and extracted from the documents. It creates a dynamic bucket based on the interval specified. In this, you can define any interval with a numeric value. This type of bucket puts in all the documents matching the criterion of the bucket whose value of the numeric field lies within the same interval as defined.

Histogram is similar to date histogram aggregation except that date histogram is used for a date/time field, whereas histogram is used for a numeric value field.

For example, if the documents contain a numeric field (quantity) holding values from 1-100, we create a dynamic bucket by specifying intervals of 10. When aggregation takes place, the quantity field of each document is computed and rounded off to the nearest bucket, meaning if the quantity is 52 and the bucket interval is 10, then it will be rounded off to 50 and thus the document will fit into the bucket associated with the key 50.

Range

This aggregation is used to specify a range size or interval of range in which each range size represents a bucket. It is used for aggregation on numeric or date/time fields. It is similar to a manual Histogram or Date Histogram aggregation. Range size has to be specified manually, which helps to analyze a subset of complete data. The range consists of from and to values.

For example, the document contains a numeric field (`user.statuses_count`) with ranges such as 1,000-3,000, 3,000-5,000, 5,000-10,000, and so on. When aggregation takes place, the values extracted from every document will be checked against every bucket range specified and the document will fit into the matching bucket, meaning there will be three buckets containing documents of users who have posted statuses in the afore-mentioned range of 1,000-3,000, 3,000-5,000, and 5,000-10,000. It is very useful for analyzing data to create clusters, such as cluster users who frequently tweet or cluster users who are popular.

> This aggregation includes the `from` value in the bucket, but excludes the `to` value for range.

Also, an upper or lower boundary can be used for creating an open range, such as `10000-*` in which this bucket will contain all documents of users who have posted statuses more than 10,000 times.

Date range

This aggregation is used to specify a range size or interval of range in date format in which each range size represents a bucket. It is used for aggregation on date/time fields. Range size has to be specified manually, which helps to analyze a subset of complete data. The range consists of from and to values.

For example, the document contains a date field (`created_at`) with ranges such as `from now-2M/M to now-1M/M` and `from now-1M/M to now`. When aggregation takes place, the values extracted from every document will be checked against every bucket range specified and the document will fit into the matching bucket, meaning there will be two buckets containing documents of a user in which bucket 1 will contain documents matching date range of current date — two months to current date — one month, and bucket 2 will contain documents matching date range of current date — one month to current date.

IPv4 range

This aggregation is used to specify a range size or interval of range in IP format in which each range size represents a bucket. The range consists of from and to values.

For example, the document contains an IP field (`host_address`) with ranges such as from `192.168.1.1` to `192.168.1.100`, from `192.168.1.100` to `192.168.1.150`. When aggregation takes place, the values extracted from every document will be checked against every bucket range specified and the document will fit into the matching bucket.

Terms

This aggregation is used to create buckets based on the values of a field. The buckets are created dynamically. It is similar to working with the GROUP BY statement used in SQL. In this, a field is specified that creates a bucket for all the values that exist in the field and puts in every document that has a value in that field.

For example, use terms aggregation on a user.languages field, which consists of languages in which a user tweets. It creates buckets for each language (**en**, **jp**, **ru**, and so on) and each bucket contains all the documents of a specific language in which a user has tweeted. So **en** language bucket will contain all documents that have been tweeted in English language and so on.

Filters

Filters are described exactly as a query, which was covered in the *Using Search Bar* section, in *Chapter 2, Exploring the Discover Page*. It is a very flexible yet powerful aggregation that helps to create visualizations based on search queries. In this aggregation, a filter is specified for each bucket on the basis of which of the documents match the filter that fits into that bucket.

For example, use filters aggregation on a field with the user.languages :(en or jp) query, which will create a bucket in which all documents containing tweets in English or Japanese fit in. If we add another filter query user.statuses_ count:[5000-*], it will create two buckets in which one bucket will contain documents of tweets in English or Japanese, and another bucket will contain documents of users who have posted statuses more than 5000 times.

 Filters aggregation is slower in execution than other aggregations.

Significant terms

This aggregation is used to find uncommonly common terms in the data present. It uses a foreground set and background set, which help to find uncommonly common words. It is useful for creating subsets of the data to analyze uncommon behaviors/scenarios. The foreground set contains the search results matched by a query (filter), and the background set contains data in the index or indices. Significant terms are used to give results that have undergone a significant change as measured between the foreground set and background set.

If a term exists in 10 documents out of 10,000 indexed documents, but appears in 8 documents from 50 documents returned from the search query, then such a term is significant.

The foreground set can be constructed by either using a query (filter) or using any other bucket aggregation, first on all documents and then choosing significant terms as sub-aggregation. The size property is used to specify how many buckets are to be constructed, meaning how many significant terms should be calculated.

For example, use filter aggregation on a field with the `user.location: India` query and select significant terms on a language field as bucket aggregation specifying size as 5. It will give the top five significant terms for the search queries that are: **en**, **hi**, and so on.

Let's understand how these results were obtained when we used significant terms. When using the search query `user.location:India`, it gave a result of 270 documents, meaning 270 documents contained the search query. When using significant terms, it gave a result of **hi** having a count of 22 out of those 270 documents. When searching for the language **hi** in all the documents, it gave a count of 160 out of the total document count of 92,004. Therefore 22/270 (8.15%) in comparison of 160/92004 (0.17%) is a significant number, which tells us how much more common **hi** is within the search query of **user.location: India** but uncommon in all the documents.

It is used to detect outliers and find anomalies. Some of the use cases are: finding trending topics on Twitter (country wise), detecting credit card fraud, and recommendation engines.

GeoHash

This aggregation is used to create buckets based on the `geo_point` fields and groups those points into buckets. The buckets are created dynamically. For this aggregation, the `geo_point` field has to be specified, which is automatically read by Kibana along with specifying precision. The smaller the precision, the larger the area covered by the buckets.

Use GeoHash aggregation on location fields to create a bucket containing tweets from users who are close to each other.

GeoHash is used with the **Tile Map** visualizations, which help to easily visualize the data on a map.

Metric aggregations

Metric aggregations are used for computing metrics over a set of documents. This aggregation is used after creating a bucket aggregation which has buckets with documents stored in it. Metric aggregation is then specified to calculate the value of each bucket, so this aggregation runs on each bucket and provides a single value result per bucket.

In the visualizations, bucket aggregation would determine the first dimension of the chart followed by the value calculated by metric aggregation, which would be termed "second dimension".

 Metric aggregations will always run on buckets, and thus would always contain bucket aggregation.

The different types of metric aggregations are as follows.

Count

This aggregation is used to return the number of documents contained within every bucket as a value. The value can be extracted from any fields present in the documents.

For example, to find out how many tweets are in each language, use a term aggregation on the `user.languages` field, which will create one bucket per language. Then use a count metric aggregation, which will display the number of tweets for each language bucket.

Sum

This aggregation is used to calculate the sum of a numeric field stored in every bucket. The result for every bucket will be the sum of all the values in that field.

Average

This aggregation is used to calculate the average value of a numeric field stored in every bucket. The result for every bucket will be the average of all the values in that field.

For example, to find out the average number of statuses of Twitter users, use a term aggregation on the `user.languages` field. Then use average metric aggregation, which will display the average number of statuses tweeted for each language bucket.

Min

This aggregation is used to calculate the minimum value of a numeric field stored in every bucket. The result for every bucket will be the minimum value for that field found in documents stored.

Max

This aggregation is used to calculate the maximum value of a numeric field stored in every bucket. The result for every bucket will be the maximum value for that field found in documents stored.

For example, to find out the maximum number of retweets in each language, use a term aggregation on the `user.languages` field, which will create one bucket per language. Then use a maximum metric aggregation on the `retweet.retweet_count` field, which will display the maximum number of retweets for each language bucket.

Unique count

This aggregation is used to count the number of unique values that exist for a field stored in every bucket. The result for every bucket will be the total number of unique values for that field found in documents stored.

For example, the documents contain a numeric field (`user.statuses_count`) with ranges such as 1,000-3,000, 3,000-5,000, 5,000-10,000 for which buckets will be created. Then, unique count metric aggregation is used on the `user.languages` field, which will display for each user the status range the number of different languages used for posting statuses.

Percentile

This aggregation is used to calculate percentiles over numeric fields stored in buckets. It is different from other metric aggregations as it stores multiple values per bucket. It comes under the category of multivalue metrics aggregation. When specifying this aggregation, a numeric value field has to be specified along with multiple percentage values. The result of this aggregation will be the value for which a specified percentage of documents will be inside the value.

For example, use percentiles aggregation on the `user.statuses_count` field and specify the percentile values as 5, 50, 75, and 95. It will result in four aggregated values for every bucket. So if we only had one single index, then the 5 percentile result will have the value of 24. This means that 5% of all the tweets in this bucket have a user status count with 24 or below. The 50 percentile result is 175, meaning that 50% of all the tweets in this bucket have a user status count of 175 or below. The 75 percentile result is 845, meaning that 75% of all the tweets in this bucket have a user status count of 845 or below. The 95 percentile result is 18500, meaning that 50% of all the tweets in this bucket have a user status count of 18500 or below.

> Both unique count and percentile are approximate calculations. They sacrifice accuracy for speed.

Percentile ranks

This aggregation is used to calculate single or multiple percentile ranks over a numeric field, which has been extracted from the documents (data) and stored in buckets. It comes under the category of multi-value metrics aggregation. It is used to display the percentage of values occurring that are below a certain specific value. If a value is greater than or equal to 75% of values occurring, it is said to be at the 75th percentile rank.

Now as we have understood all the aggregations provided in Kibana, let's understand how to use these aggregations with visualizations.

Steps for designing visualization

To create a new visualization, we follow a step-by-step process that can be initiated by clicking on the **Visualize** tab, which is the second tab at the top of the page.

> If you are already creating a visualization, you can create a new visualization by clicking on the New Visualization button , which is present in the toolbar just to the right of the search bar.

Step 1 – selecting a visualization type

It lists the different visualization types with an option to select any one of the following:

Area Chart	Use **Area Charts** to visualize the total contribution of several different series. The areas can be displayed as stacked, overlap, percentage, wiggle, or silhouette.
Data Table	Use **Data Tables** to display tables of aggregated data stored in Elasticsearch.
Line Chart	Use **Line Charts** to display the aggregated data in the form of lines. The lines can be displayed on a scale of linear, log, or square root.
Markdown widget	Use **Markdown widget** to display any type of information or instructions related to dashboard.
Metric	Use the **Metric** visualization to display a single number on your dashboard for various metric aggregations.
Pie Chart	Use **Pie Charts** to display each source's contribution to a total. It can be displayed as a pie or as a donut.
Tile Map	Use **Tile Maps** to display a map for results based on GeoHash aggregation, which requires a `geo_point` field.
Vertical Bar Chart	Use **Vertical Bar Charts** as a general-purpose chart. The bar chart can be displayed as stacked, percentage or grouped.

When clicking on the **Visualization** tab to create a new visualization, you will see the following options as shown in the following image:

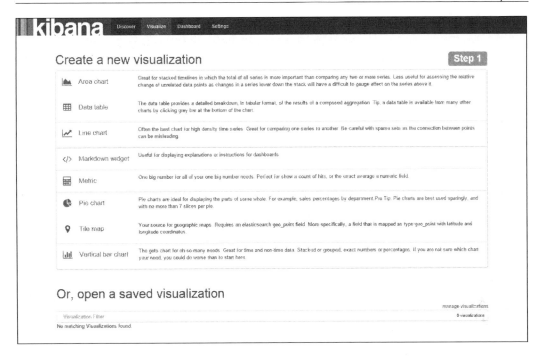

In this figure, you have various selection options to create a new visualization, or you can also load a saved visualization (if created earlier). We will discuss the saved visualizations in the *Save Visualization* section in this chapter.

If the new visualization is of the **Markdown widget** type, then selecting it will take you to a text entry field where you can enter the information or any text that you require. If you select any other visualization type, you will be taken to step 2.

Step 2 – selecting search data source

This step is used to select the search source on the basis of which you would visualize. You can either select a new search or a saved search as the data source for creating visualizations. All the searches are associated with an index or bunch of indices.

You have two options to select a search source:

- From a new search
- From a saved search

When you select from a new search and have multiple indices defined, then you would be given a drop-down menu to select the index on which you want to visualize. It is used to create visualizations based on stored data.

When you select from a saved search, it will link the visualization with the search query saved on the **Discover** page. As the search is linked with visualization, any changes made to the search, the visualization will be automatically updated.

You will see the following options to select a search source as shown in the following figure:

In this figure, you can see the option of choosing a search source from either a new search or a saved search. Upon selecting either of them, you will be taken to step 3.

Step 3 – the visualization canvas

This step is very important as it enables you to create, edit, and configure visualizations. The main elements of the visualization canvas are:

1. Toolbar
2. Aggregation designer
3. Previewing visualization

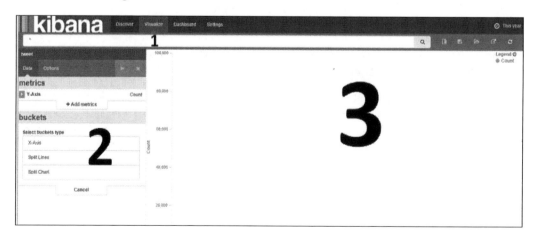

Toolbar

The toolbar is used for powerful analysis of data based on search queries and filters. It is used for specifying the search query on the basis of which visualization changes and updates automatically. It has a search field that is used for interactive searching of data along with controls to create, save, or load visualizations. The toolbar consists of a search bar along with option buttons such as New Visualization, Save Visualization, Load Saved Visualization, Share Visualization, and Refresh.

 For visualizations created using saved search (described in step 2), the search bar is grayed out and displays, **This visualization is linked to a saved search**. Double-click on it to unlink the visualization from saved search providing you with an option to edit the search.

New Visualization

New Visualization provides the option to create a new visualization. It erases the present visualization and creates a new one to play with. It is done by clicking on the New Visualization button , which is situated on the toolbar beside the search bar:

Save Visualization

Save Visualization provides the option of saving a created visualization. It is used to save the current created visualization along with the selected index information. This option is situated beside the New Visualization button on the toolbar.

To save a visualization, perform the following steps:

1. Create a visualization.

2. Click on the Save Visualization button  present on the toolbar next to the New Search button:

3. Give it a title to save.

4. Click on **Save** to save the visualization.

Load Saved Visualization

Load Saved Visualization provides the option of loading any previously created and saved visualization. It is used to load visualization with a specified index. If loading a saved visualization included a different index, then on loading it, the selected index also gets updated. This option is situated beside the Save Visualization button on the toolbar.

To load a saved visualization:

1. Click on the Load Saved Visualization button  present in the toolbar next to the Save Visualization button:

2. Specify the saved name to load it. All the saved visualization filters are displayed below the search bar.

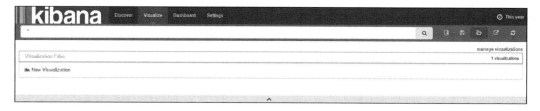

3. Click on it to load the saved visualization.

Share Visualization

Share Visualization provides the option of sharing your visualization, which is either created or saved and can be shared among the people to view. It also provides the option of either sharing the link to your visualization or embedding the visualization within any HTML page (which would still require access to Kibana for viewing). This option is situated beside the Save Visualization button in the toolbar.

To share visualization, perform the following steps:

1. Click on the Share Visualization button ![icon] present in the toolbar next to the Save Visualization button:

2. Upon clicking on it, you will find a link for embedding this visualization and sharing the visualization:

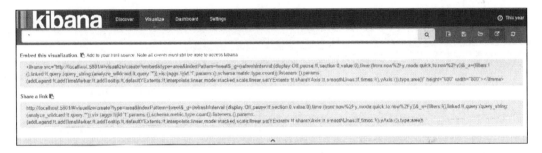

3. Click on the copy to clipboard button ![icon] beside **Share a link** to copy the link and share it. Otherwise, you can copy to clipboard button beside **Embed this visualization**, and paste the `iframe` source into an HTML page to display visualizations in a webpage/application.

Refresh

The refresh button is used to refresh the page.

Aggregation designer

This is the heart of creating visualizations. It is displayed on the left-hand side of the **Visualize** page. It is used for configuring the metric and bucket aggregations as discussed previously, which is used for visualizations. Buckets are similar to SQL Group By statements. The aggregation builder consists of two tabs:

- **Data**: this is used for specifying the metric and bucket aggregations. Metric aggregations include count, average, sum, min, max, standard deviation, unique count, percentile, and percentile ranks. Bucket aggregations include date histogram, histogram, range, date range, IPv4 range, terms, filters, and significant terms.

  For each different type of visualization we have different types of metrics and bucket options, which are described briefly in the following table:

Type of visualization	Metrics	Bucket
Area Chart	Y-axis	X-axis, split area, split chart
Data Table	Metric	Split rows, split table
Line Chart	Y-axis	X-axis, split lines, split chart
Metrics	Metric	-
Pie Chart	Slice size	Split slices, split chart
Tile Map	Value	Geo coordinates, split chart
Vertical Bar Chart	Y-axis	X-axis, split bars, split chart

  You can set the order of execution for each bucket. The re-ordering of buckets changes the order of execution.

   In Kibana, the first aggregation becomes the base data set for subsequent aggregations.

- **Options**: this is used to display the various types of view options associated with each type of visualization. Each visualization created has its own view options to change a few aspects. These are optional and have options that can be selected or de-selected as per requirements. It provides flexibility in creating different types of visualizations. Some of the options associated with visualizations are briefly stated in the following table:

Type of visualization	View options
Area Chart	Chart mode (stacked, overlap, percentage, wiggle, silhouette), smooth lines, set Y-axis extents, scale Y-axis to data bounds, show tooltip, show legend
Data Table	Per page, show metrics for every bucket/level, show partial rows
Line Chart	Y-axis scale (linear, log, square root), smooth lines, show connecting lines, show circles, set Y-axis extents, scale Y-axis to data bounds, show tooltip, show legend
Metric	Font size
Pie Chart	Donut, show tooltip, show legend
Tile Map	Map type (scaled circle markers, shaded circle markers, shaded GeoHash grid, Heatmap), desaturate map tiles
Vertical Bar Chart	Bar mode (stacked, percentage, grouped) set Y-axis extents, scale Y-axis to data bounds, show tooltip, show legend

To see the visualization on a preview canvas, click on the green Apply Changes button ▣ at the top right of the aggregation builder, beside the two tabs of **Data** and **Options**.

Preview canvas

Preview canvas is used to display a preview of the visualization created using the aggregation designer. Whenever the aggregation designers apply changes with different sets of metrics, options are automatically displayed on the preview canvas.

An explanation of visualization types

Now, after understanding the aggregations and the various steps of designing a visualization, let's explore each visualization type in detail, with working examples to make things easier to understand. In the following explanation, only step 3 would be used as defined previously, namely visualization canvas.

Area Chart

This is used to display areas below the lines and is similar to Line Charts. It is also used to display data over a period of time.

The chart that we would like to create would show a comparison of top languages in which users tweeted, along with the retweet count for those languages over a period of time. In this we will split the chart on the basis of top languages, split the area on the basis of `retweet.retweet_count`, and the X-axis will contain the period of time:

1. Firstly, specify the metrics on the Y-axis as count (though it's not limited; it can use any other metric as per requirements).

2. Then we add a new split chart bucket type and add aggregation of terms specifying the field language with top 2 size. After adding this, we have split the chart, showing the amount of tweets in the top 2 languages tweeted by users.

3. Then we will add a **Split Area** sub-bucket and add sub-aggregation of terms specifying the field `retweet.retweet_count` with top 3 size. After adding this we have split the area showing the top 3 retweet counts in the top 2 languages tweeted by users.

4. As **Area Charts** are used to display data over a period of time we will add an X-axis sub-bucket, having the sub-aggregation as **Date Histogram** using the `created_at` field with the interval of minute.

5. Finally, we have a visualization that shows the top 3 retweet counts for the top 2 languages in which users have tweeted.

 While using Area Charts you may encounter the following error message: **Area charts require more than one data point. Try adding an X-Axis aggregation**. It shows an error as an X-axis is required as input for providing visualizations in the **Area Chart**. Also, an error can occur if the Time Filter selected does not fit into the visualization.

To preview the visualization, click the green Apply Changes button ▶ to update your visualization or click the grey Discard Changes button ✕ to discard changes to the visualization.

Whenever you are adding/modifying buckets, aggregations, sub-aggregations or options, click the aforementioned buttons to update/discard visualizations.

You can see the output in the form of a screenshot, shown as follows:

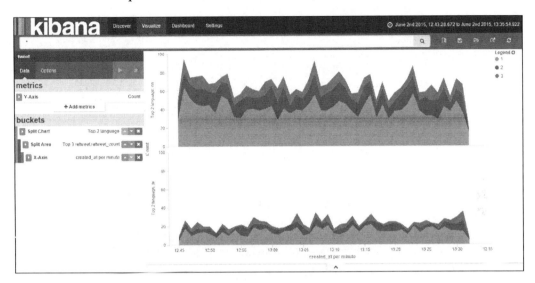

In the previous screenshot, **Chart Mode** is stacked (by default), which shows all the documents across the buckets from the height of the stacked elements.

Let's save this visualization as **Area Chart**, which will be used in *Chapter 4, Exploring the Dashboard Page*.

 Split Chart by default splits in rows, but it can also be split into columns by selecting columns just underneath the **Split Chart** bucket.

In the **Options** tab, by default **Chart Mode** is set as stacked but can be changed to other chart modes by selecting the following chart modes.

Overlap

In this view, areas would not be stacked upon each other; instead every area will begin at the X-axis and would be displayed in a semi-transparent way so that all areas are seen properly. It makes it easier to see the values of different buckets but difficult to get a total value of all the buckets:

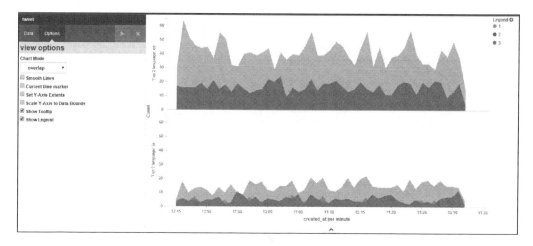

Percentage

In this **Chart Mode**, the height of the chart will always be shown as 100% and the count for each bucket will be displayed in terms of the percentage of the whole chart.

For example, at a particular time (June 2, 12:46) we have 64 as the retweet count of 1, 16 as the retweet count of 2, and 15 as the retweet count of 3, so in percentage mode we will show a 64 retweet count along with 67.4%, meaning [(64 / 95) * 100] where 95 = 64 + 16 + 15:

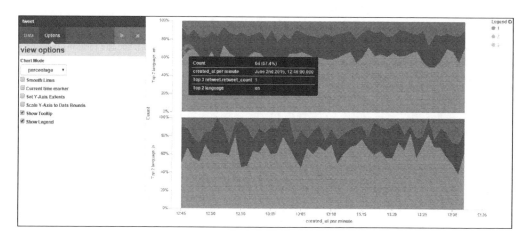

Wiggle

This **Chart Mode** displays the aggregation as a stream graph, which is a stacked area graph displaced around a central axis resulting in a flowing shape:

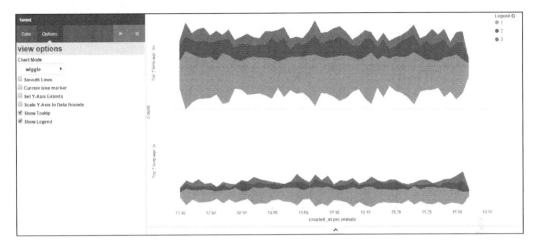

Silhouette

This **Chart Mode** displays the aggregation as a variance from the central line from which chart evolves in both directions:

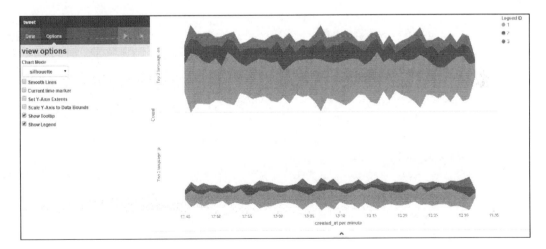

Every string field specified in buckets, aggregation, or sub-aggregations have customization options, which can be edited/used by clicking on the **Advanced** button shown beneath **Order By**, and include the following options:

- **Exclude Patterns**: This specifies a pattern to exclude from the results
- **Exclude Pattern Flags**: These are a set of java flags for exclusion pattern
- **Include Patterns**: This specifies a pattern to include in the results
- **Include Pattern Flags**: These are a set of java flags for inclusion pattern
- **JSON Input**: This adds specific JSON properties to merge with aggregation

> Advanced options as described would be available to edit/use for every string field used in either of the buckets, aggregation, or sub-aggregations across all visualizations.

Also, other view options alter the following behavior of **Area Charts**:

- **Smooth Lines**: Check this box to curve the top boundary from point to point:

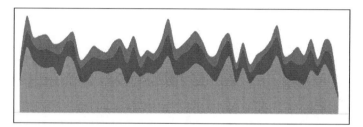

- **Current Time Marker**: Check this box to draw a red line on current time data
- **Set Y-Axis Extents**: Check this box to specify y-max and y-min fields to set specific values for the Y-axis
- **Scale Y-Axis to Data Bounds**: Check this box to change upper and lower bounds to match values returned in data
- **Show Tooltip**: Check this box to enable information when hovering over visualization
- **Show Legend**: Check this box to view the legend that is shown next to the chart

Data Table

Data Table is used to display a table of aggregated data stored in Elasticsearch. It provides raw data results in tabular format.

The **Data Table** that we would like to create would show the top languages along with a count of each language's retweets in the ranges of 0 to 10 and 10 to 20. In this, we will split the rows on the basis of top languages and split the rows on the basis of the `retweet_count` ranges:

1. Firstly, specify the metrics as count (though not limited to it, can use any other metric as per requirement).

2. Then we add a new **Split Rows** bucket and add aggregation of terms specifying the field language with top 5 size. After adding this, we created a **Data Table** showing a count of tweets in the top 5 languages tweeted by users.

3. Then we will add a **Split Rows** sub-bucket and add **Range** sub-aggregation, specifying the field `retweet.retweet_count` with ranges from 0 to 10 and 10 to 20.

4. Finally, click on the **Apply Changes** button to view the visualization, which shows `retweet_count` ranges for the top 5 languages in which users have tweeted.

You can see the output in the form of a screenshot, as follows:

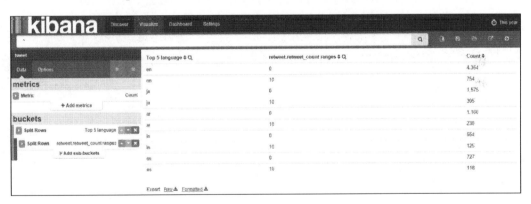

Let's save this visualization as a **Data Table**, which will be used in *Chapter 4, Exploring the Dashboard Page*.

In the **Options** tab, there are view options that alter the following behavior of **Data Table**:

- **Per Page:** This is used for pagination of the table. By default, 10 rows are displayed per page. This option can be changed as per requirements.

- **Show metrics for every bucket/level**: Check this box to display the intermediate metrics result corresponding to each bucket aggregation.

- **Show partial rows**: Check this box to display rows even if there is no result.

Line Chart

This is used to display the aggregated data in the form of lines. The lines can be displayed on a linear, log, or square root scale. It is also used to display data over a period of time.

The chart that we would like to create would show the comparison of top languages in which users tweeted, along with the retweet count for those languages over a period of time. In this, we will split the chart on the basis of top languages, split the area on the basis of `retweet.retweet_count`, and the X-axis will contain the period of time:

1. Firstly, specify metrics on the Y-axis as count (though it's not limited, it can use any other metric as per requirement).

2. Then we add a new **Split Chart** bucket and add aggregation of terms specifying the field language with top 2 size. After adding this, we have split the chart showing the count of tweets in the top 2 languages tweeted by users.

3. Then we will add a **Split Lines** sub-bucket and add sub-aggregation of terms specifying the `retweet.retweet_count` tweet with top 3 size. After adding this, we have split the area showing the top 3 retweet counts in the top 2 languages tweeted by users.

4. As **Line Charts** are used to display data over a period of time, we will add an X-axis sub-bucket, having sub-aggregation as date histogram, using the field `created_at`, with minute intervals.

5. Finally, click on the **Apply Changes** button to view the visualization, which shows the top 3 retweet counts for the top 2 languages in which users have tweeted.

You can see the output in the form of a screenshot, as follows:

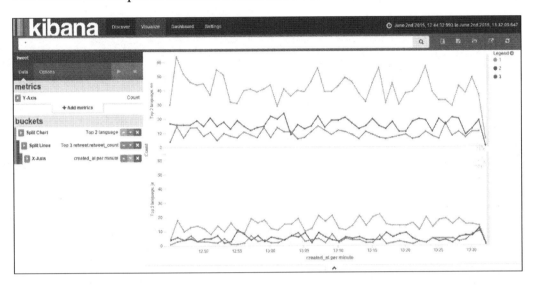

In the previous screenshot, the Y-axis scale is linear (by default), which displays the Y-axis scale as the count of matching documents.

Let's save this visualization as **LineChart**, which will be used in *Chapter 4, Exploring the Dashboard Page*.

In the **Options** tab, by default, the Y-axis scale is set as linear but can be changed to other scales by selecting the following scale options.

Log

In this option, the Y-axis scale calculates its values based on the logarithm of the count value. It is used to display data exponentially:

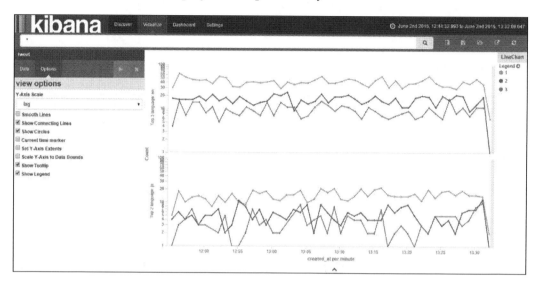

Square root

In this option, the Y-axis scale calculates its values based on the square root of the count value:

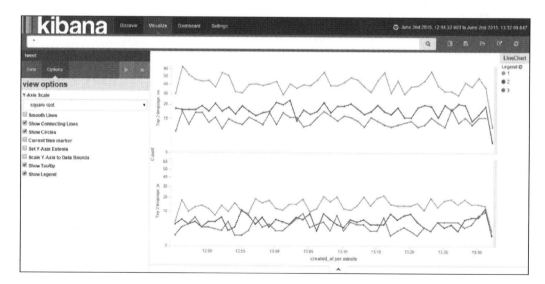

Also, other view options alter the following behavior of **Line Charts**:

- **Smooth Lines**: Check this box to curve the top boundary from point to point:

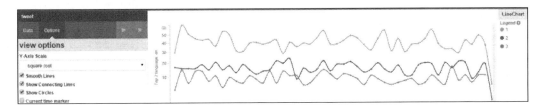

- **Show Connecting Lines**: Check this box to draw lines between points
- **Show Circles**: Check this box to draw each data point as a circle:

- **Current Time Marker**: Check this box to draw a red line on current time data
- **Set Y-Axis Extents**: Check this box to specify y-max and y-min fields to set specific values for the Y-Axis
- **Scale Y-Axis to Data Bounds**: Check this box to change upper and lower bounds to match values returned in data
- **Show Tooltip**: Check this box to enable information when hovering over the visualization
- **Show Legend**: Check this box to view the legend that is shown next to the chart

There is a new variation to **Line Charts** known as **Bubble Charts**. **Bubble Charts** are used to display data points as bubbles.

You can convert a **Line Chart** visualization to a **Bubble Chart** visualization by using the following steps:

1. Create a **Line Chart** visualization or load a created **LineChart** visualization.
2. In **Data** tab, under **Metrics**, click on **Add Metrics** and select metrics type as **Dot Size**, and specify **Dot Size Ratio** and **Aggregation** as **Count** (or choose any other).

3. In the **Options** tab, uncheck the **Show Connecting Lines** box and click on the **Apply Changes** button.

Let's save this visualization as **Line_Bubble**, which will be used in *Chapter 4, Exploring the Dashboard Page*.

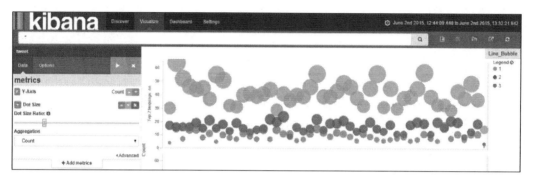

Markdown widget

This is a text entry field used to input any type of information or instructions. It is useful in displaying the text, links, code, tables, and so on, entered on the dashboard, which acts as additional information and can be used easily. Kibana renders the text entered and displays the result on the dashboard. It does not have any relation to visualization using your data.

The markdown is a GitHub-flavored markdown. There is a help link that, upon clicking, takes you to the help page for a GitHub-flavored markdown.

Metric

Metric visualization is used to display a single number for various metric aggregations. In this, no bucketing is done, the metrics aggregations are applied to the complete data set, meaning the index on which visualizations are being created. The data set can be changed either by choosing another index or querying in the search bar.

It is easy to create by just clicking on the **Add Metrics** and select **Metrics**. Then select the aggregation followed by the field name (if aggregation is chosen as count specifying field, a name is not required).

Let's create a very interesting **Metric** visualization to calculate the unique hashtags in the data set and determine the preferred length of hashtag for Twitter. For this we would require the following inputs:

- Total data set count
- Unique count of hashtags (unique count of the `hashtag.text` field)
- Minimum hashtag start position (minimum of the `hashtag.start` field)
- Minimum hashtag end position (minimum of the `hashtag.end` field)
- Maximum hashtag start position (maximum of the `hashtag.start` field)
- Maximum hashtag end position (maximum of the `hashtag.end` field)
- Average hashtag start position (average of the `hashtag.start` field)
- Average hashtag end position (average of the `hashtag.end` field)

Let's save this visualization as **Metrics**, which will be used in *Chapter 4, Exploring the Dashboard Page.*

Finally, click on the **Apply Changes** button to view visualization as shown in the following screenshot:

From the previous screenshot, we have analyzed the average hashtag length based on 13,695 unique hashtags received. It states an average of approximately 11 characters for hashtags used by users.

This type of analysis can easily be done by companies in order to determine the length of hashtag for trending on Twitter.

Pie Chart

This is used to display each source's contribution to the total. It can be displayed either as a pie or as a donut. It is most useful for displaying the parts of some whole. Pie charts use slices; fewer slices is easier to visualize.

The chart that we would like to create would show comparison of top languages in which users tweeted, along with top country code for those languages over a period of time. In this we will split the chart on the basis of `created_at`, split slices on the basis of top languages, and split slices on the basis of top country code. In **Pie Charts**, **Split Charts** are generally used before **Split Slices**:

1. Firstly, specify metrics on **Slice Size** as **Count** (though it's not limited, it can use any other metric as per requirement).

2. Then we add a new **Split Chart** bucket and add aggregation of date histogram on field `created_at` with the interval of hourly. After adding this, we have split the chart on the basis of hours.

3. Then we will add a **Split Slices** sub-bucket and add a sub-aggregation of terms specifying the field language with top 5 size. After adding this, we have split the slices in **Pie Chart** showing the top 5 languages on an hourly basis.

4. To display the top country code for those languages, we will add a **Split Slices** sub-bucket with sub-aggregation as terms specifying the field `place.country_code` with top 2 size.

5. Finally, click on the **Apply Changes** button to view the visualization, which shows the top 5 languages along with the top 2 country codes for those languages by hourly intervals.

You can see the output in the form of a screenshot, as follows:

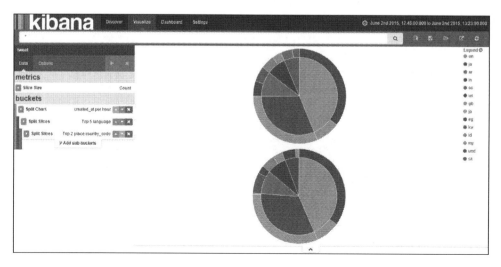

In the previous screenshot, pie charts are split by hourly intervals (as we have data of the 12th hour and 13th hour). Each pie chart is split by the top 5 languages (shown as the inner pie) and each language is split by the top 2 country codes from which users have tweeted (shown as the outer pie). The size of each pie is determined by the count of matching documents in every bucket.

The size in percentage is computed as follows:

For the 12th hour, English language contains United States (US) and Great Britain (GB) as the top 2 countries that have tweeted in the English language. If the total count of tweets by US and GB for English language is 156, out of which the US has 126 tweets, then their slice percentage is equal to (126 / 156) * 100 = 80.77%, and GB has 30 tweets, then their slice percentage is equal to (30 / 156) * 100 = 19.23%. It is shown in the following screenshot:

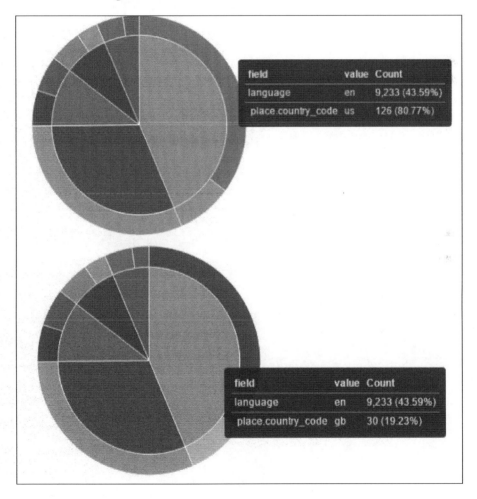

Splitting charts without splitting slices is not supported.

Let's save this visualization as **PieChart**, which will be used in *Chapter 4, Exploring the Dashboard Page*.

In the **Options** tab there are view options that alter the following behavior of pie charts:

- **Donut**: Check this box to view pie charts in the shape of a donut

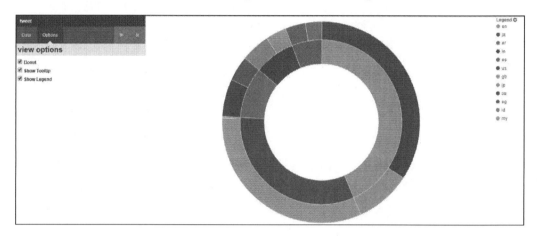

- **Show Tooltip**: Check this box to enable information when hovering over visualization
- **Show Legend**: Check this box to view the legend that is shown next to chart

Tile Map

This is used to display GeoHash type aggregation results over the map. It requires a `geo_point` type field with inputs of latitude and longitude. It uses **Geo Coordinates** bucketing. The visualization would display the data points captured in the form of circles (by default) where size will depend upon the precision chosen, and color is signified by the actual value calculated by whichever metric aggregation was used.

We would like to map the locations of the countries from which users have tweeted. In this we will use **Geo Coordinates** in a bucket.

1. Firstly, specify metrics on **Value** as **Count** (though it's not limited, it can use any other metric as per requirement).

2. Then we add a new **Geo Coordinates** bucket and add aggregation of GeoHash specifying the field location. After adding this, we will see a map that has circles as data points captured by the location field.

3. Finally, click on the **Apply Changes** button to view the visualization, which shows the location on a map from which users have tweeted.

You can see the output in the form of a screenshot, as follows:

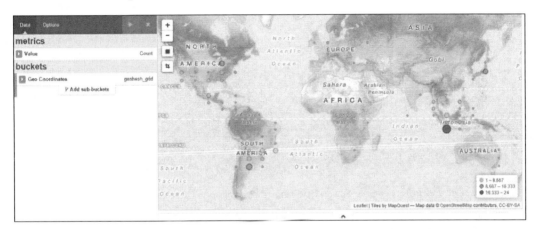

In the previous screenshot, the **Map type** is **Scaled Circle Markers**, which scales the size of the markers (data points) based on the metric aggregation's value. The size of each circle varies based on the range of metric value.

Let's save this visualization as **Map**, which will be used in *Chapter 4, Exploring the Dashboard Page*.

Upon importing sample Twitter data, you will not be able to create the Tile Map visualization as it will return an error stating that no field found matching the geo_point type. In the GitHub repository, within the Readme file, there are steps to fetch twitter data using elasticsearch Twitter river using which sample twitter data was generated and further exported to a sample file using elasticdump utility.

In the **Options** tab, by default, **Map type** is set as **Scaled Circle Markers** but can be changed to other map types by selecting the following options:

Shaded Circle Markers

In this option, the size of each circle varies with the location of latitude and longitude. The closer to the equator, the smaller the circle size, and the further from the equator, the larger the circle size. It is used to display the markers (data points) with different shades based on the metric aggregations' value:

Shaded GeoHash Grid

In this option, markers (data points) are displayed using rectangular cells of GeoHash grid instead of the circles as shown in the previous images. It is used to display the markers (data points) with different shades based on the metric aggregations' value.

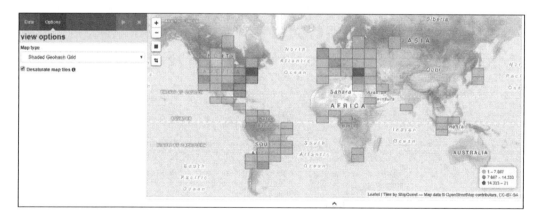

Heatmap

This is a special kind of tile map, which is a two-dimensional graphical representation of data having values displayed using colors instead of numbers, text, or markers (data points). It provides an easy way to understand and analyze complex/huge data sets. It applies blurring of markers and shading (dark or light) on the basis of the total amount of overlap.

Heatmap contains the following properties:

- **Radius**: This is used to set the size of all Heatmap dots occurring on the map. The larger the radius, the bigger the size of overlap of dots; the smaller the radius, the smaller the size of overlap of dots. By default it is 25.

- **Blur**: This is used to set the blurring amount for all Heatmap dots occurring on the map. The higher the blur, the fewer individual Heatmap dots are shown; the lower the blur, the more individual Heatmap dots are shown. By default it is specified as 15.

- **Maximum Zoom**: This is used to define the zoom level of the map at which all Heatmap dots are displayed at full intensity. The higher the zoom, the more the intensity of dots; the lower the zoom, the less the intensity of dots. In Kibana tile maps, maximum zoom is supported up to 18 zoom levels. By default it is specified as 16.

- **Minimum Opacity**: this is used to set the opacity for all Heatmap dots. By default it is specified as 0.1.

- **Show Tooltip**: check this box to enable information when hovering over visualization.

Desaturate map tiles

It is used to desaturate the map color so that the colors appear more clearly. It does not work on any version of **Internet Explorer** (IE).

The following figure shows Heatmap with the **Desaturate map tiles** check box ticked:

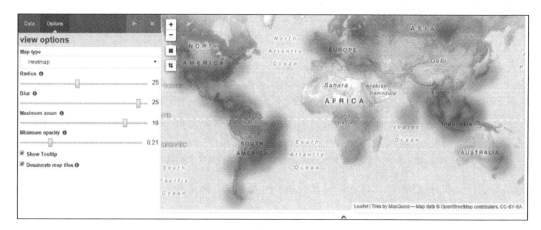

The following figure shows Heatmap with the **Desaturate map tiles** not ticked:

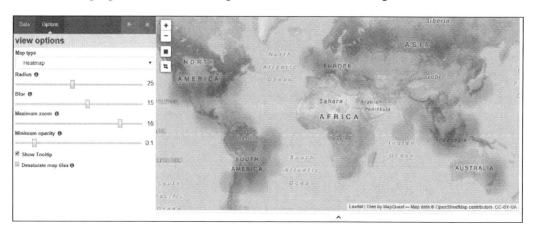

Also, after creating the **Tile Map** visualization, we can explore the map in the following ways:

- Click-and-drag the cursor anywhere on the map to move the map center
- Click on the Zoom In/Out buttons ⁺₋ to change the zoom level

- Click on the Draw a Rectangle button ▣ to create a filter for the box coordinates by drawing a rectangle box
- Click on the Fit Data Bounds button ▣ to automatically adjust the map and display the map boundaries according to the GeoHash bucket that has at least a single result

Vertical Bar Chart

This acts as a general-purpose chart suited to both time-based data and non-time-based data. The bar chart can be displayed either as stacked, percentage, or grouped. In this type of chart, every X-axis value will have its own corresponding bar where the size of every bar signifies the metric aggregation.

The chart that we would like to create will show the comparison of the top languages in which users tweeted, along with the retweet count for those languages over a period of time. In this, we will split the bars on the basis of the top languages, split the chart on the basis of `retweet.retweet_count`, and the X-axis will contain the period of time:

1. Firstly, specify the metrics on the Y-axis as count (though it's not limited, it can use any other metric as per requirement).
2. Then we add a new X-axis bucket, having aggregation as date histogram using the field `created_at` with the interval of minute. After adding this, we will get a count of tweets on a per minute basis in terms of a histogram.
3. Then we will add a **Split Bars** sub-bucket and add sub-aggregation of terms specifying the field language with top 2 size. After adding this, we have split the bar showing the top 2 languages which have been tweeted by users on a per minute basis.
4. To display the range of retweet count for the top 2 languages we will add a **Split Chart** sub-bucket having sub-aggregation as **Range** specifying the field `retweet.retweet_count` with the ranges defined as from 0 to 5 and from 5 to 10.
5. Finally, click on the **Apply Changes** button to view the visualization, which shows tweets from users on a per minute basis, specifying the top 2 languages in which users have tweeted, along with splitting the bar chart on the basis of the retweet count range.

 While using bar charts you may encounter the following error message: **This container is too small to render the visualization**. It shows an error as the visualization created using the buckets cannot fit into the preview visualization canvas.

You can see the output in the form of the screenshot, as follows:

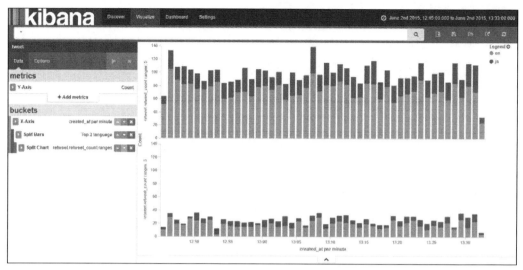

In the previous screenshot, the bar mode is stacked (by default), which shows all the documents across the buckets from the height of the stacked elements.

Let's save this visualization as **BarChart**, which will be used in *Chapter 4, Exploring the Dashboard Page*.

In the **Options** tab, by default, **Bar Mode** is set as stacked but can be changed to other bar modes by selecting the following bar modes.

Percentage

In this bar mode, the height of the bar will always be shown as 100% and the count for each bucket will be displayed in terms of percentage of the whole bar.

For example, at a particular time (June 2, 12:45) we have 52 as the retweet count in range 0 - 5 for the English language, and 12 as the retweet count in range 0 - 5 for Japanese, so in percentage mode we will be shown 52 retweet counts along with 81.3%, meaning [(52 / 64) * 100] where 64 = 52 + 12:

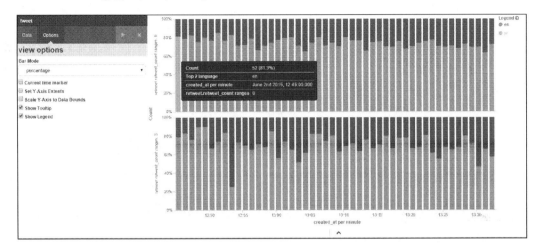

Grouped

This bar mode groups the results of each bucket and displays them alongside each other:

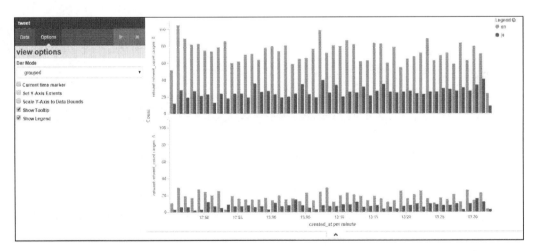

Also, other view options alter the following behavior of bar charts:

- **Current Time Marker**: Check this box to draw a red line on current time data
- **Set Y-Axis Extents**: Check this box to specify the y-max and y-min fields to set specific values for the Y-axis
- **Scale Y-Axis to Data Bounds**: Check this box to change upper and lower bounds to match values returned in data
- **Show Tooltip**: Check this box to enable information when hovering over visualization
- **Show Legend**: Check this box to view the legend, which is shown next to the chart

Summary

In this chapter, we learned about the various types of aggregation provided by Elasticsearch in Kibana. It provided an insight into the importance of using aggregations for visualizing data in Kibana. It was followed up with explanation of the different types of visualization present in Kibana, along with a detailed explanation of each type of visualization and its options.

In the next chapter, we will learn about the usage of the **Dashboard** page in Kibana, along with using the visualizations created to easily form a beautiful dashboard. We will explore how Kibana provides an easy way to form dashboards, along with instant sharing and embedding of dashboards.

4
Exploring the
Dashboard Page

Dashboard is one of the pages present in Kibana 4 that provides you with a single page for you to use your saved visualizations. It is used to combine the different types of visualizations created and display them on a single page. The visualizations added to the dashboard can be arranged in any way as per the user's requirements. They can easily be moved, resized, edited, and removed. This page is very useful as it displays all types of visualizations created, which makes data easier to understand rather than going through the data itself.

The advantages of the **Dashboard** page in Kibana are as follows:

- It provides a single view page for visualizations, that caters to a business' need
- It is easier to understand data visually rather than having to interpret raw data
- It is easy to use visualizations on multiple dashboards without coding
- The dashboard and visualizations are updated automatically as more data flows in
- Editing the visualization will update the changes in all dashboards that use that visualization
- You can filter the dashboard based on search queries, which will change the visualizations in a dashboard as per the search results
- You can create filters by clicking on any visualization

 To create a dashboard, there should be at least one saved visualization.

When you open the **Dashboard** page, you will be greeted with the following empty Kibana dashboard:

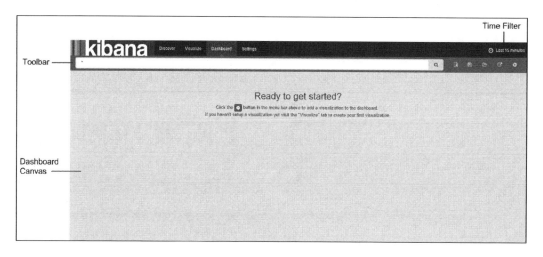

As shown in the preceding image:

- The time filter contains data about a particular time interval.
- The toolbar consists of a search bar along with these options: New Dashboard, Save Dashboard, Load Saved Dashboard, and Share and Add Visualization.
- The dashboard canvas is used to display the added visualizations. Also, when the dashboard is empty, it states **Click on the add button** **to add a visualization to the dashboard**.

> Make sure that the time filter is correct. By default, it is set to the last 15 minutes.

In this chapter, we are going to take a look at the following topics:

- Adding visualizations to dashboard
- Saving a dashboard
- Customizing visualizations in dashboard
- Embedding a dashboard into a web page
- Explanation of debug panel

To understand these topics in a better way, let's explore the **Dashboard** page.

Understanding the toolbar

The toolbar is an important component of the **Dashboard** page as it provides various options to deal with visualizations. The search bar is used to specify the search query or filters that are used to analyze a visualization. Whenever a search query is specified, it checks in all the documents and return the results of the search query. The existing visualizations are updated as per the search query results obtained. The toolbar consists of a search bar along with option buttons such as New Dashboard, Save Dashboard, Load Saved Dashboard, and Share and Add Visualization.

Let's understand the usage of the different options of the toolbar in detail.

The New Dashboard option

New Dashboard provides the option to start adding visualizations to an empty dashboard. It empties the visualizations created and added to the dashboard. It also empties the current dashboard. This is done by clicking on the New Dashboard button which is situated on the toolbar, beside the search bar, as shown in the following screenshot:

> If you have added visualizations to a dashboard and without saving it if you click on New Visualization, then the added visualizations will be gone. You will need to add those visualizations again.

Adding visualizations

The Add Visualization option provides the option of adding visualizations to the dashboard. You can add as many saved visualizations as you want. When using an empty dashboard, you can click on the add button from the dashboard canvas or the add button situated at the end of the toolbar beside the share button.

To add a visualization, perform the following steps:

1. Click on the Add Visualization button, as shown here:

2. Specify the name of the saved visualization that you want to add, as shown in the following screenshot:

 You can search for a visualization by typing the name in the **Visualization Filter** field, which will filter as per the search.

3. The visualization that you select will appear on the dashboard canvas within a container.

Let's create a dashboard by adding saved visualizations (saved in *Chapter 3, Exploring the Visualize Page*).

We will add the following saved visualizations:

- **AreaChart**
- **PieChart**
- **LineChart**
- **BarChart**
- **Line_Bubble**

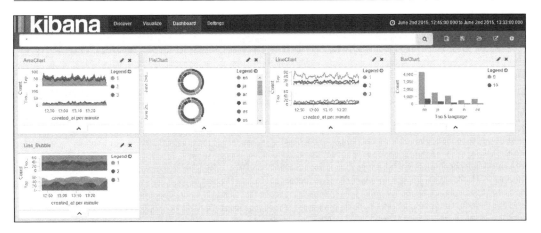

The dashboard created in the preceding screenshot does not look visually beautiful, nor is it interesting to view at a glance. To make this dashboard look attractive, we will explore more customization options in the *Understanding the dashboard canvas* section.

> You can also add saved searches into dashboards. They can be added by clicking on the add button and selecting a saved search from the searches tab, which is present beside the **Visualizations** tab. Saved searches are represented in the dashboard by the document data, which shows filtered results as per the search query.

Using the search bar

After adding visualizations, we can query the dashboard in a similar way to how we queried in *Chapter 2, Exploring the Discover Page*. As per the search query entered, all the relevant visualizations will be updated with the result of the search query. This is a crucial functionality provided in Kibana, which makes it easier to analyze data and monitor the data/trends for different requirements.

The Save Dashboard option

The Save Dashboard option provides the option of saving a dashboard. It is used to save the visualizations that are currently added to the dashboard. This option is situated beside the New Dashboard button in the toolbar.

To save a dashboard, follow these steps:

1. Click on the Save Dashboard button ![save icon] present in the toolbar next to the New Dashboard button, as shown here:

2. Give this dashboard a name to save with. We will use Kibana_Dashboard as the name to save our dashboard:

3. Click on **Save** to save the dashboard. Whenever any changes are made to the dashboard, you need to save it.

 If you select the checkbox for **Store time with dashboard** then it will save the time filter along with the visualizations. Whenever you load this saved dashboard, the time filter will automatically be changed.

The Load Saved Dashboard option

The Load Saved Dashboard option provides the option of loading a saved dashboard. It is used to load a dashboard that contains visualizations. This option is situated beside the save dashboard button on the toolbar.

To load a saved dashboard, perform the following steps:

1. Click on the load saved dashboard button ![load icon] present on the toolbar, next to the Save Dashboard button, as shown in this screenshot:

2. Specify the saved dashboard name to load it. All saved dashboards are displayed below the search bar.

3. Click on the name of the saved dashboard to load it, as shown in the following screenshot:

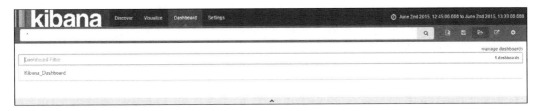

Sharing the saved dashboard

The Share option provides the option of sharing your saved dashboard among people who wish to view it. It also provides the option of either sharing the link of your dashboard or embedding the dashboard within any HTML page (which would still require access to Kibana for viewing). This option is situated beside the load saved dashboard button on the toolbar.

To share a dashboard, follow these steps:

1. Click on the share button  on the toolbar, next to the load saved dashboard button, as shown here:

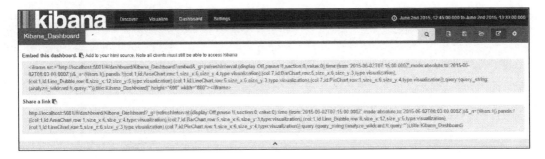

2. Upon clicking on it, you will find the link for embedding this dashboard and sharing it, like this:

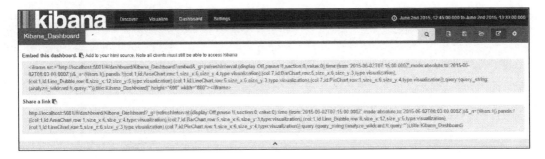

3. Click on the copy to clipboard button 📋 beside **Share a link** to copy the link and share it. Alternatively, you can copy the clipboard button beside **Embed this dashboard** and paste the `iframe` source in an HTML page to display visualizations in a web page/application.

Later in this chapter, in the *Embedding Dashboard in a web page* section, an example of how to embed a dashboard in a simple web page will be shown.

Understanding the dashboard canvas

The dashboard canvas provides a preview of all saved visualizations added to the dashboard. As every added visualization appears on the dashboard canvas within a container, we will explore various ways of customizing these containers. By customizing these containers, we can easily create a beautiful visualization.

Moving visualizations

In a dashboard, you can rearrange the added visualizations as per your liking. We can move the container that has visualizations anywhere in the dashboard.

To move containers, perform these steps:

1. Click and drag the container title bar (heading) using the mouse.
2. Release the button where you wish to confirm the new location for the visualization.

 While you are moving a container, other containers will shift as per the size of the moving container.

Resizing visualizations

In a dashboard, you can also resize the added visualizations as per your liking. You can resize the container containing visualizations anywhere in the dashboard.

To resize containers, perform the following steps:

1. Move your mouse pointer to the bottom-right corner of the container until your pointer changes to indicate the resize option at the corner.
2. Click and drag to resize the visualization.
3. Release the button where you wish to confirm the new size of the visualization.

Editing visualizations

Furthermore, in a dashboard, you can edit existing visualizations.

To edit a visualization, perform these steps:

1. Click on the edit visualization button ✎ on the title bar of the container.
2. You will be taken to the visualization canvas page, where you can edit it.
3. After editing, click on the save visualization button. The saved visualization will automatically be updated on the dashboard.

Removing visualizations

You can remove existing visualizations from a dashboard. This provides you with the flexibility to create a dashboard as per your required visualizations and delete unnecessary visualizations.

 If you are removing visualizations, please remember that this does not delete the underlying visualization, but only removes the link to the visualization from the dashboard.

To remove a container, click on the remove container button 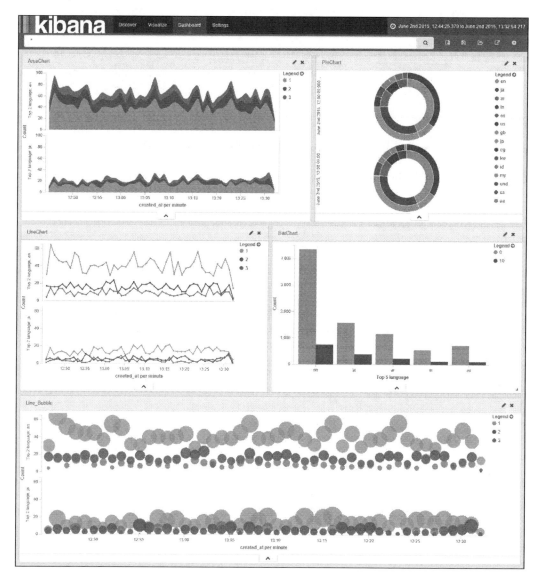 present on the title bar of the container.

After using the aforementioned customizing options, we have transformed the dull-looking dashboard into a visually beautiful dashboard, as shown in the following screenshot:

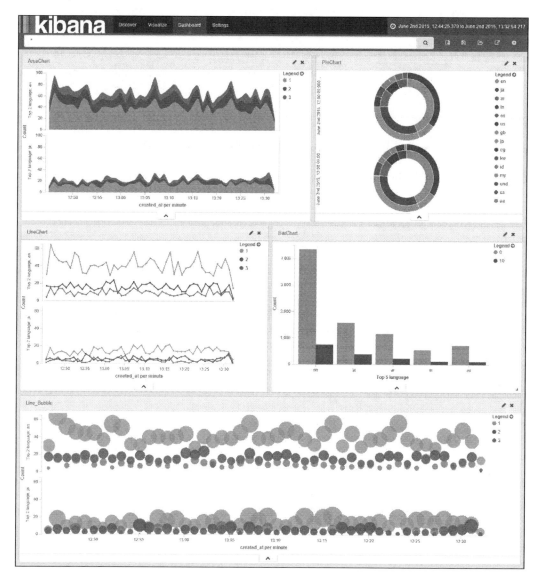

The preceding dashboard provides a beautifully crafted visualization that can easily be analyzed instead of analyzing a huge amount of raw data. Trends can easily be understood using various types of charts, as you can see.

 By default, all dashboards in Kibana 4 are stored in the .kibana index. If you delete this index (manually or by clearing all indexes in Elasticsearch) then all your saved searches, visualizations, and dashboards will be lost.

Embedding a dashboard in a web page

We will use the saved dashboard and click on the copy to clipboard button beside **Embed this dashboard** option to copy the link for embedding. We will create a simple HTML file and use this iframe source to embed it in a web page:

```
<html>
<head>
<title> Kibana_Embed</title>
</head>
<body>
<center><b>Have a look at the functionality of embed in Kibana 4.1 </
b></center>
<iframe src="http://localhost:5601/#/dashboard/Kibana_
Dashboard?embed&_a=(filters:!(),panels:!((col:1,id:AreaChart,row:
1,size_x:6,size_y:3,type:visualization),(col:7,id:BarChart,row:5,
size_x:6,size_y:3,type:visualization),(col:1,id:Line_Bubble,row:8,
size_x:12,size_y:5,type:visualization),(col:1,id:LineChart,row:5,
size_x:6,size_y:3,type:visualization),(col:7,id:PieChart,row:1,si
ze_x:6,size_y:3,type:visualization)),query:(query_string:(analyze_wi
ldcard:!t,query:'*')),title:Kibana_Dashboard)&_g=(refreshInterv
al:(display:Off,pause:!f,section:0,value:0),time:(from:'2015-06-
02T07:15:00.000Z',mode:absolute,to:'2015-06-02T08:03:00.000Z'))"
height="600" width="800"></iframe>
</body>
</html>
```

In the preceding HTML file, we added an iframe source that contains different visualizations added to the dashboard in which we can customize properties such as (though not limited to) rows, *x* axis, *y* axis, height, and width for every visualization.

The HTML page that we just described looks like this:

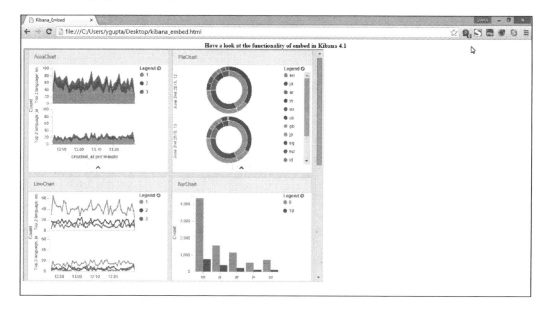

 Elasticsearch and Kibana should be running in order to access embedded visualizations. Besides, you can share and embed individual dashboards and visualizations.

Understanding the debug panel

The debug panel is used to view the raw data of Elasticsearch behind a visualization. It will give us detailed information, such as the results of the visualization and what the request of Elasticsearch was, along with the response from Elasticsearch, and the statistics behind it.

To view the debug panel, click on the caret (^) button. It is at the bottom of each visualization.

Let's take a look at the debug panel with **Bar Chart** created in *Chapter 3, Exploring the Visualize Page*, which shows the top five languages that have `retweet.retweet_count` in the ranges of 0-10 and 10-20.

Table

Table represents the data behind the visualization in the form of a table. This table contains data in the form of pages. You can sort this data by clicking on any of the headers of the columns, as shown here:

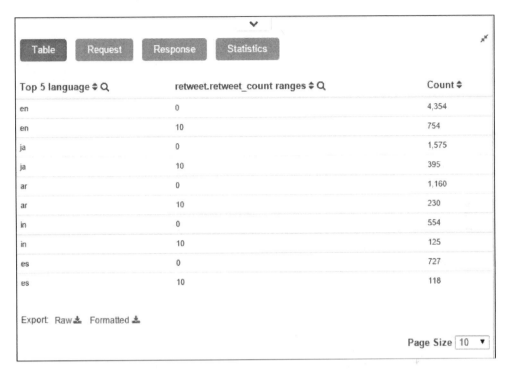

In the preceding screenshot, you can view the raw data underlying the visualization. You can even change the **Page Size** value to accommodate the results in one page. Also you can export the tabular form data in either raw form or formatted form, which is exported as a CSV file.

Request

Request represents the raw request sent to Elasticsearch as a query, which is in a JSON format. It displays the Elasticsearch request body, which can be directly queried from Elasticsearch for the created visualization:

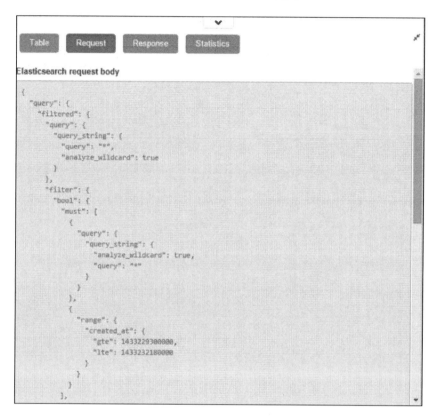

Response

Response represents the raw response received from Elasticsearch as the result of the request query, which is in a JSON format. It displays the Elasticsearch response body, which is the result of the query for the created visualization obtained from Elasticsearch:

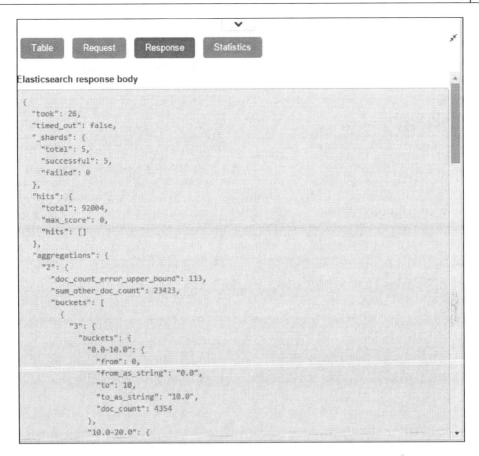

Statistics

Statistics represents the statistics used for the query in a tabular format, such as **Query Duration**, **Request Duration**, **Hits** (the total number of records), and **Index**, as shown here:

Query Duration	26ms
Request Duration	327ms
Hits	92004
Index	"tweet"

The debug panel can also be accessed from the **Discover** page (at the bottom of the histogram) and the **Visualize** page (at the bottom of the visualization).

Summary

In this chapter, we covered the advantages of using dashboards in Kibana. This was followed by an explanation of the various components of the **Dashboard** page. This chapter then provided an insight into the importance of using the **Dashboard** page to create beautiful dashboards, by combining various visualizations and customizing each of them to fit into a single panel. It also taught you how to embed a dashboard within a web page.

In the next chapter, you will understand the **Settings** page in Kibana. We will explore how to customize and tweak the basic and advanced settings used in Kibana.

5
Exploring the Settings Page

The **Settings** page is one of the pages present in Kibana 4 that helps you customize and tweak the various settings provided in order to use Kibana efficiently. This page gives you a full overview of the different types of indices present wherein you can configure as many index patterns as you want, followed by the advanced settings in which, settings that are either undocumented, unsupported, or experimental can be tweaked, along with managing and editing saved objects such as **Dashboards**, **Searches**, and **Visualizations**.

> Use advanced settings very carefully, changing it can have unintended outcomes.

The **Settings** page contains the following tabs:

* **Indices**
* **Advanced**
* **Objects**
* **About**

In this chapter, we will go through all of these tabs in brief. Let's explore these tabs and understand the settings provided for each of them.

Indices

The **Indices** tab is used to edit settings related to the index. Within this tab, you can configure/add an index pattern, set any index as default, and remove the index pattern. You can also view information related to every field and edit the field properties.

Configuring an index pattern

Indices is the default tab that opens whenever you start Kibana or click on the **Settings** page. As Elasticsearch uses an index to process data, it remains the most important component, without which we cannot analyze data, create visualizations, or build dashboards. Index is the heart of Elasticsearch and Kibana.

It displays the following information when opened:

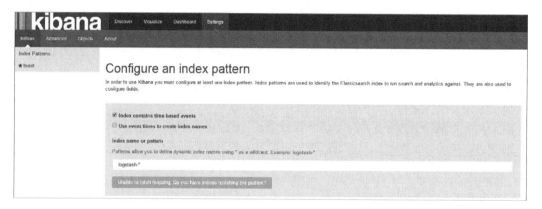

By default, an index contains time-based events that are ticked. If your data does not contain any time-based event, then you can uncheck the checkbox in order to configure an index.

> If your index does not contain the time-stamped field, then uncheck the Index contains the **time-based events** option to add index to Kibana. When viewing the **Discover** page, the histogram will not be displayed, though all the document data will be shown.

While configuring indices, you can use patterns such as * (asterisk), which matches zero or more characters.

For example, suppose you have indices such as **kibana-**, **kibana-1**, **kibana-2**, and **kibana-10**, each containing five documents in every index.

In this, you can use the * pattern and define the index pattern as **kibana-***, which will read all the aforementioned indices and add them for use in Kibana. In Kibana, Indices tab will show a single index under the index pattern **kibana-***, and under this index, all the matching indices documents will be shown; that is, the **kibana-*** index will contain 20 documents:

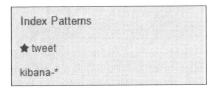

 Searching for indices using wildcard patterns is an inefficient way of searching. For example, if you are searching only for the last 15 minutes of data but are using the **kibana-*** index pattern in your query, you are forcing Elasticsearch to consult all the indices to check whether they contain any data.

You can also use the date format pattern to add indices that have the event times/timestamp attached to it.

For example, suppose you have indices such as **kibana1-2015-08-12**, **kibana1-2015-07-27**, and **kibana1-2015-06-02**.

To define the event times, tick the **Use event times to create index names** option. Upon clicking on it, you will see the following options to define:

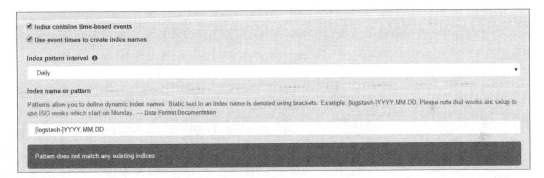

In this, you can define **Index pattern interval**, which defines how frequently the index is created and can be chosen as **Hourly**, **Daily**, **Weekly**, **Monthly**, or **Yearly**.

Then, define the index pattern as **[kibana1-]YYYY-MM-DD**, which will read all the aforementioned indices and add them for use in Kibana:

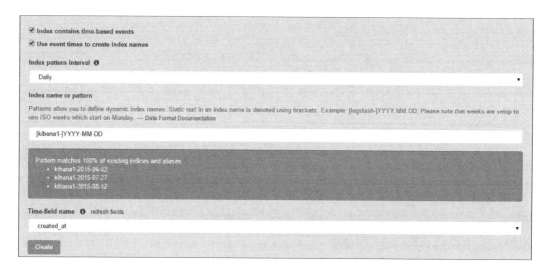

It displays the added index pattern on the left, under **Index Patterns**, as shown in this screenshot:

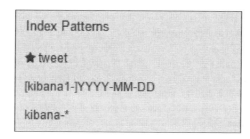

 Searching for indices using this pattern is much more efficient than searching for them using the wildcard pattern, that is, the **kibana-*** index pattern.

For additional properties related to an index, click on the index to view the following options:

Setting the default index pattern

The default index pattern is used to automatically select an index for use in the **Discover** tab. The default index selected is used to view data in the **Discover** tab. Kibana puts a star just before the name of the index as listed in **Index Patterns**. The first index created is, by default, selected as the default index.

To change the default index pattern:

1. Click on the index name that you want to set as default under **Index Patterns**.

2. Click on the favorite button ![star] to set it as the default index.

Reloading the index fields list

Kibana automatically retrieves the index along with the fields associated with the index from Elasticsearch. Reloading the index fields list provides the flexibility to include newly added fields in the index by reloading the index. Reloading the index resets the popularity counter for fields, which shows the fields that are most often used by the user.

To reload the index fields list:

1. Click on the index name under **Index Patterns** for which you want to reload the field.

2. Click on the reload button [⟳] to reload the field list.

Removing an index pattern

This feature is used to remove an index pattern added to Kibana.

To remove an index pattern:

1. Click on the index name that you want to delete under **Index Patterns**.

2. Click on the delete button [🗑] to remove the index pattern.

Managing the field properties

After you click on the index name along with additional properties as explained earlier, more customizations are provided for editing each field property. Let's explore the information provided by the fields:

*   **Name**: This displays the name of the field.
*   **Type**: This displays the type of the field and whether it contains a date, number, string, or geo-point.
*   **Format**: This displays the format of the type of field. For every field type, we can set the format. The supported formats for each field type are mentioned here:

Field type	Supported formats
String	URL and string
Number	URL, bytes, number, percentage, and string
Date	URL, date, and string
Geo_point	String
Boolean	URL and string

- **Analyzed**: This indicates whether the field is analyzed or not. The analyzed fields are tokenized into single words; that is, if a string contains multiple words, they are broken into single words. For example, if a string contains United Kingdom and it is an analyzed field, then it will be tokenized as United and Kingdom. If the field is not analyzed, it will not be tokenized and will remain as a single word.

- **Indexed**: This indicates whether the field is indexed or not.

The field type format

To change the format of the field type, click on the pencil button 🖉 under the heading of controls. Let's explore the various supported formats in detail:

- **String**: This is used to apply the following transformations to the field:
    - **Lower case**: This converts the text in field to lowercase.
    - **Upper case**: This converts the text in field to uppercase.
    - **Short dots**: This replaces the content before the . (dot) character with the first character.

      For example, change the format of the text field to **string** and transform into **upper case**.

      After you have selected the transformation, click on the **Update Fields** button to reflect the changes. As you can see here, the result to the left was obtained using the default options, while the screenshot to the right was obtained after transforming to uppercase:

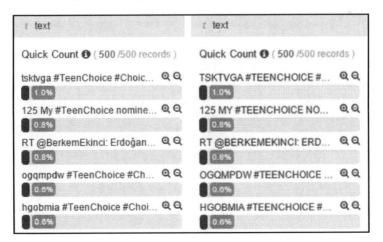

- **URL**: This is used to apply the following types to the field:
    - **Link**: This is used to convert the text in the field into a URL.
    - **URL Template**: This is used to add text/values to the link. It provides `{{value}}`, which gives the `url-escaped` values, and `{{rawValue}}` gives the values in raw form as its input.
    - **Label Template**: This is used to replace the URL with any text string.
    - **Image**: This is used to specify the image directory in which the images are located.

      For example, let's change the format of the text field to **URL** and specify the type as `Image`. Enter **URL Template** as `{{rawValue}}` (by default, if this is empty, it is set to `rawValue`). Enter **Label Template** as **User Image**.

      As you can see here, the screenshot to the left was obtained using the **Default** options, while the screenshot to the right was obtained using the link options:

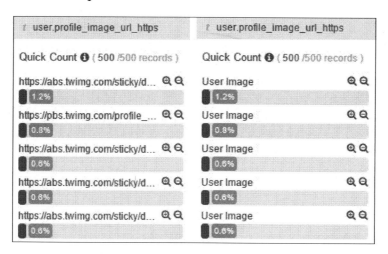

 If you add this field by clicking on **Add** beside the column name, then you will be able to see images corresponding to the user profile images.

- **Date**: This is used to display the timestamp using the moment.js format pattern. By default, the pattern is MMMM DD YYYY, HH:mm:ss.SSS.

  Here is an example, change the format of the text field to **Date** and input the pattern as DD-MMM-YYYY HH:mm:ss.SSS.

  Again, the screenshot to the left was obtained using the **Default** options, while the screenshot to the right was obtained after changing the **Default** options:

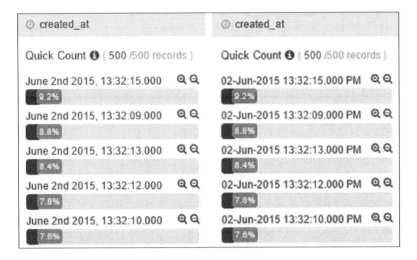

- **Number**: This is used to display numbers using the **numeral.js** format pattern. By default, the pattern is 0,0.[000].

- **Bytes**: This is also used to display numbers using the numeral.js format pattern. By default, the pattern is 0,0.[000]b.

- **Percentage**: This too is used to display numbers using the numeral.js format pattern. By default, the pattern is 0,0.[000]%.

 After you've clicked on an index in the **Fields** tab, beside it, you will see a number. This number denotes the total number of fields in an index.

Advanced

This tab is for advanced users. It provides the options of editing the settings that directly control the Kibana application. The settings can be undocumented, unsupported, or experimental. Tweaking the settings can cause unexpected behavior.

To set **Advanced Settings**, perform the following steps:

1. Go to **Settings | Advanced**.

2. Click on the edit button for the option that you want to edit.

3. Enter a new value.

4. Click on the save button .

A few examples are given here:

- **Changing discover**: The sampleSize option shows the number of rows in a table. The default is **500**; change it to **100**. Now scroll to the bottom of the **Discover** page.

These are the first 500 documents matching your search, refine your search to see others. Back to top.
These are the first 100 documents matching your search, refine your search to see others. Back to top.

- **Changing the histogram**: The barTarget option is used to try to generate the number of bars when there is a specified auto-interval in the date histogram. By default, it is **50**; change it to **10**. Now go to the **Visualize** page and create a date histogram.

  As shown here, the screenshot on top was obtained using the default options while the screenshot below it was obtained after changing the default options:

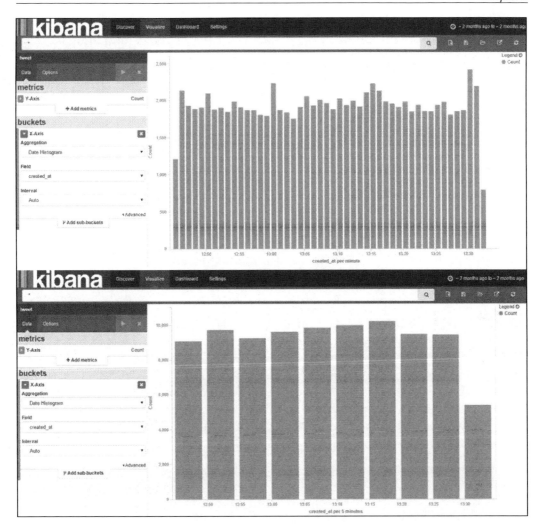

- **Changing the csv:separator option**: This is used to separate exported values. By default, it is , (comma); change it to : (colon).

- **Changing the csv:quoteValues option**: This is used to define whether the value should be quoted when CSV is exported. The default is `true`; change it to `false`.

  Now open the saved **Data Table** visualization and export the data in the **Raw** format.

The screenshot to the left was obtained using the default options, while the screenshot to the right was obtained after changing the default options:

```
"Top 5 language","retweet.retweet_count ranges",Count    Top 5 language:retweet.retweet_count ranges:Count
en,"0.0-10.0",4354                                       en:0.0-10.0:4354
en,"10.0-20.0",754                                       en:10.0-20.0:754
ja,"0.0-10.0",1575                                       ja:0.0-10.0:1575
ja,"10.0-20.0",395                                       ja:10.0-20.0:395
ar,"0.0-10.0",1160                                       ar:0.0-10.0:1160
ar,"10.0-20.0",230                                       ar:10.0-20.0:230
in,"0.0-10.0",554                                        in:0.0-10.0:554
in,"10.0-20.0",125                                       in:10.0-20.0:125
es,"0.0-10.0",727                                        es:0.0-10.0:727
es,"10.0-20.0",118                                       es:10.0-20.0:118
```

Objects

This tab is used to view, edit, delete, export, and import saved objects, such as saved searches, saved visualizations, and saved dashboards.

Managing saved searches, visualizations, and dashboards

This provides an advanced setting in which modification of an existing saved object can be done. It enhances the reusability of created searches, visualizations, or dashboards. The objects can be viewed, edited, deleted, exported, or imported into Kibana. To manage saved objects, go to **Settings | Objects**. The following page will be displayed:

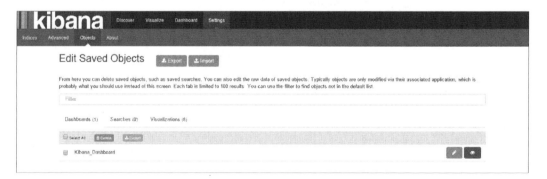

Viewing a saved object

In this setting, it provides a single page to view all the saved objects. The saved objects can be viewed in the **Objects** tab which is under the **Settings** page. If you have saved a search in the **Discover** page, it will be listed inside the **Searches** tab. If you have saved a visualization in the **Visualize** page, it will be listed inside the **Visualizations** tab. If you have saved a dashboard in the **Dashboard** page, it will be listed inside the **Dashboards** tab.

To view a saved object, follow these steps:

1. Click on the **Settings** tab, followed by the **Objects** tab.
2. All the saved objects will be displayed within the respective tabs.
3. Click on the selection box to select the object that you want to view.
4. Click on the view button .

Editing a saved object

With the setting of editing a saved object, Kibana provides the flexibility to directly alter the object description, the object metadata, the object saved name, and the JSON that specifies all the properties of the object.

To edit a saved object, perform the following steps:

1. Click on the **Settings** tab, followed by the **Objects** tab.
2. All the saved objects will be displayed within the respective tabs.
3. Click on the selection box to select the object that you want to edit.
4. Then click on the edit button ![edit] .
5. Make changes to the object name, description, metadata, or object properties.
6. Click on the save object button Save visualization Object .

> Directly clicking on the name of the saved object will lead you to edit the saved object page.

Deleting a saved object

With this setting, you can delete any created or saved object. It provides an easy way to directly delete saved objects.

To delete a saved object, follow these steps:

1. Click on the **Settings** tab and then on the **Objects** tab.
2. All the saved objects will be displayed within the respective tabs.
3. Click on the selection box to select the object that you want to delete.
4. Then click on the delete button **🗑 Delete** .

Exporting saved objects

Once you do this setting, you can easily export saved objects and they can be reused whenever needed. By exporting saved objects, a backup can easily be maintained, which can be used if the object gets deleted or corrupted.

To export a saved object, perform the following steps:

1. Again, click on the **Settings** tab and then on the **Objects** tab.
2. All the saved objects will be displayed within the respective tabs.
3. Click on the selection box to select the object that you want to export.
4. Click on the export button **⬇ Export** and specify the location to save the object exported in JSON format at.

Importing saved objects

With this setting you can easily import saved objects providing the ability to reuse whenever needed.

To import saved objects:

1. Click on the **Settings** tab, followed by the **Objects** tab.
2. Click on the import button to import the saved object.
3. Specify the filename to be imported, which contains the saved object JSON data.
4. Click on **Open** after choosing the file.

If you import an object that already exists, you will be asked whether you want to overwrite the existing object or not.

About

This tab provides a few details of Kibana, such as the running **Version**, the **Build** number, and **Commit SHA**. This page can be viewed by going to **Settings | About**, and it displays the following information:

Summary

In this chapter, we covered the various basic and advanced settings provided in Kibana. Initially, we covered how to configure the index pattern, followed by setting the default index, deleting the index pattern, and customizing the various properties of fields. This was followed by tweaking advanced settings. This can break the software if not used properly. Finally, we covered how to manage saved searches, visualizations, and dashboards, including viewing, editing, deleting, exporting, and importing saved objects.

In the next chapter, which is also the final chapter of this book, we will see how to use Kibana for real-time Twitter data analysis and create beautiful visualizations for different scenarios.

6
Real-Time Twitter Data Analysis

After understanding the various components of Kibana, let's explore in detail how to use Kibana to analyze and visualize data for real-world scenarios. In this chapter, we will see an end-to-end workflow of how to fetch Twitter data, along with storing data in Elasticsearch. This will be followed by building beautiful visualizations in Kibana to examine various scenarios.

The two possible ways of fetching Twitter data directly into Elasticsearch are by using:

- Elasticsearch Twitter river
- Logstash Twitter input

> Note that Twitter river is available as a plugin. It can be used to fetch tweets using Elasticsearch and Kibana only. To use Twitter input, Logstash is required along with Elasticsearch and Kibana. Both ways allow you to fetch Twitter data easily.

We will use Logstash Twitter input because rivers acting as plugins in Elasticsearch have become deprecated; that is, they will be removed in future versions of Elasticsearch.

Before we move further, let's understand Logstash in brief.

Logstash is an open source tool created by Jordan Sissel. He later joined Elasticsearch, which was renamed Elastic. It is a data collection tool aimed at fetching events for processing. Events are nothing but data containing a timestamp field in it. Logstash is responsible for processing events by connecting with various input sources and storing data in various output sources. It helps combine data from multiple sources and parses it by applying filters to modify the incoming data.

The main purposes of using Logstash are to read event data from different kinds of input sources (these can be a file, HTTP, GitHub, Elasticsearch, and so on), apply filters to transform and process the incoming events (these can be parsing, encoding JSON, aggregation, and so on), and send processed events to the destination source (this can be CSV, a file, CloudWatch, Elasticsearch. and so on).

Logstash can be described in brief as:

```
Input -------> Filter ---------à Output
```

The various input plugins available in Logstash are shown here:

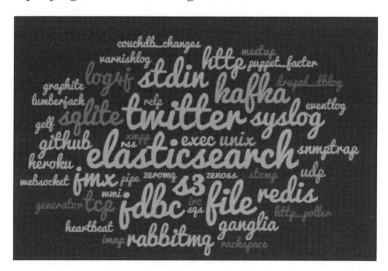

The various filter plugins available in Logstash are as follows:

Finally, the various output plugins available in Logstash are shown in the following image:

In this chapter, we are going to take a look at the following topics:

- The installation of Logstash
- The workflow for real-time Twitter data analysis
- Creating a Twitter developer account
- Creating a Logstash configuration file
- Creating visualizations for scenarios

The installation of Logstash

In this section, Logstash will be installed. Logstash 1.5.4 will be installed, and the section covers the installation on Ubuntu and Windows separately.

The installation of Logstash on Ubuntu 14.04

To install Logstash on Ubuntu, perform the following steps:

1. Download Logstash 1.5.4 as a tar file using the following command in the terminal:

    ```
    curl-L -O http://download.elastic.co/logstash/logstash/logstash-
    1.5.4.tar.gz
    ```

2. Extract the downloaded `.tar` file using the following command:

    ```
    tar -xvzf logstash-1.5.4.tar.gz
    ```

    This will extract the files and folder into the current working directory.

3. Navigate to the `bin` directory within the `logstash-1.5.4` directory:

    ```
    cd logstash-1.5.4/bin
    ```

4. To check whether Logstash has been installed successfully, type the following command in the terminal after navigating to the `bin` folder:

    ```
    logstash --version
    ```

    This will print the Logstash version installed.

The installation of Logstash on Windows

We can install Logstash on Windows by going through and applying the following steps:

1. Download the latest version of Logstash from the Elastic site using the following link:

    ```
    curl-L -O http://download.elastic.co/logstash/logstash/logstash-
    1.5.4.zip
    ```

2. Extract the downloaded `.zip` package by either unzipping it using WinRAR, 7-Zip, and so on (if you don't have any of these software, download any one of them), or using the following command in GIT Bash:

    ```
    unzip logstash-1.5.4.zip
    ```

    This will extract the files and folder into the directory.

3. Then, click on the extracted folder and navigate through the folder to get to the `bin` folder.

4. To check whether Logstash has been installed successfully, type the following command in command prompt after navigating to the `bin` folder:

   ```
   logstash --version
   ```

   This will print the Logstash version installed.

The workflow for real-time Twitter data analysis

In this section, we will cover the end-to-end workflow of how to fetch tweets using Logstash and visualize tweets with Kibana.

The workflow for real-time Twitter data analysis will be as follows:

- Creating a Twitter developer account to get keys to fetch tweets
- Creating a Logstash configuration file that specifies the input and output
- Fetching tweets using the Logstash Twitter input
- Storing tweets in Elasticsearch using the Logstash Elasticsearch output
- Analyzing Twitter data and creating visualizations in Kibana for scenarios

This analysis can be performed for a wide range of activities, such as marketing, brand building, brand management, customer focus, and so on. In this chapter, we will focus on how a company can use Twitter to build their brand and get unique statistics related to it using Twitter. Also, this would be useful for a company to monitor their marketing campaigns.

At the end of this chapter, you will be able to answer questions such as these:

- How many times has my brand been tweeted about in a time interval?
- Which are the top languages in which people tweet about my brand?
- Which are the different geographical locations from where people are tweeting about my brand?
- From which devices are people mostly tweeting about my brand?
- In which languages, from different devices, are people tweeting about my brand?
- From which countries, using different devices, are people tweeting about my brand?

- What are the top retweeted user screen names related to my brand tweeting from different devices?

- What are the top user screen names tweeting about my brand?

- What are the most popular hashtags related to my brand?

After getting answers to the preceding questions, it will become easier for a company to analyze its brand and get crucial information such as the devices used by its customers, the top countries where its customers talk about its product, the top usernames, the top retweeted usernames, and the most popular hashtags used for its brand.

Creating a Twitter developer account

In this section, we will cover the process of creating a Twitter developer account. It is required for fetching tweets to authorize and authenticate the application with Twitter, through which data will be fetched.

To create a Twitter developer account, perform the following steps:

1. Go to www.twitter.com and log in with your Twitter username and password. If you do not have a Twitter account, sign up by entering your name, e-mail ID, and a password.

2. After creating or signing in to your account, add your mobile number to your Twitter profile before you create a Twitter application. Your mobile number can be added by clicking on your profile image and selecting **Settings**. Then, select the **Mobile** option on the left-hand side and provide your mobile number. Next, click on **Continue**. It will then send a one-time password to validate your account, which you will receive on your provided mobile number. You will see the following page for adding your mobile number:

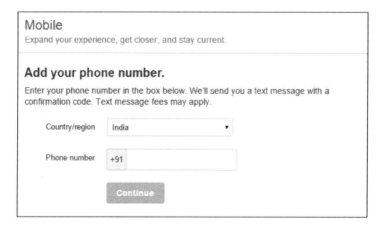

3. Go to the Twitter application web page by entering the URL `www.dev.twitter.com/apps`. Here, you will see a list of all the applications created using your Twitter login credentials.

4. To create a new application, click on **Create New App**. You will see this web page:

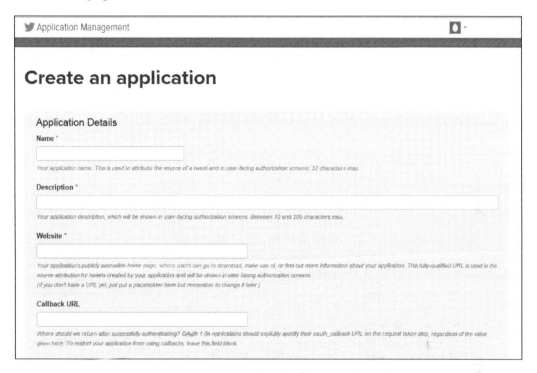

It will ask you to fill in the following details to create an application:

> **Name**: You have to provide a unique name for your Twitter application. The name has to be unique or else you will get an error that this particular name has already been taken.

> **Description**: You have to provide a description of your Twitter application. This provides brief information about your Twitter application. It has to be a minimum of 10 characters.

Website: You have to provide a website that will act as the home page for your Twitter application. However, we are using it for personal use—for fetching tweets. So, provide any website address or put a placeholder. The website has to be specified with http or https followed by the domain name, for example, `http://www.twitter.com`.

Callback URL: This is used when you are allowing the user to sign in to your application to authenticate themselves. This URL is where they will be returned after they've offered consent to Twitter to use your application. It is optional.

After filling in the preceding details, read the **Developer Agreement** and tick the **Yes, I agree** checkbox. Click on the **Create your Twitter application** button to create your app.

After successful creation of your application, **Consumer Key** and **Consumer Secret Key** will be generated automatically.

5. Now you have to create the access token. It will allow your Twitter application to read data from Twitter, including tweets and information about them. Go to the **Keys and Access Tokens** tab, scroll down the web page, and click on the **Create my access token** button. Then, mention the access type for this Twitter application.

   It will automatically create your **Access Token** and **Access Token Secret Key**. Refresh the page if you do not see the newly created access tokens.

6. Now, click on the **Keys and Access Tokens** tab to view your **Consumer Key (API Key), Consumer Secret (API Secret), Access Token**, and **Access Token Secret values**, which will look like this:

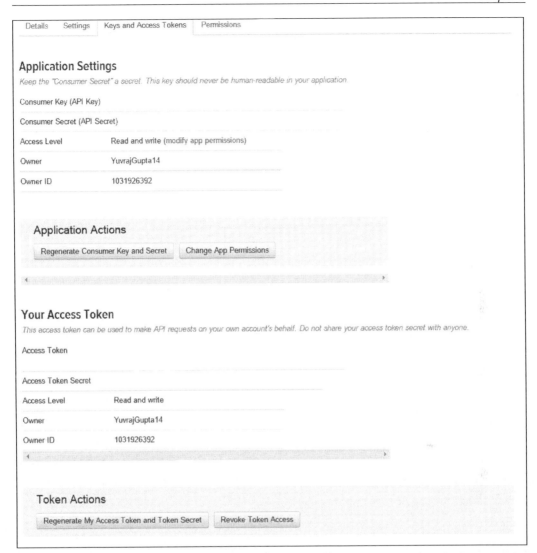

| Details | Settings | Keys and Access Tokens | Permissions |

Application Settings

Keep the "Consumer Secret" a secret. This key should never be human-readable in your application.

Consumer Key (API Key)

Consumer Secret (API Secret)

Access Level	Read and write (modify app permissions)
Owner	YuvrajGupta14
Owner ID	1031926392

Application Actions

[Regenerate Consumer Key and Secret] [Change App Permissions]

Your Access Token

This access token can be used to make API requests on your own account's behalf. Do not share your access token secret with anyone.

Access Token

Access Token Secret

Access Level	Read and write
Owner	YuvrajGupta14
Owner ID	1031926392

Token Actions

[Regenerate My Access Token and Token Secret] [Revoke Token Access]

 I have removed the keys of my Twitter application for security reasons.

Creating a Logstash configuration file

In this section, we will develop a configuration file that will contain input and output. Here, input will be twitter and output will be elasticsearch, as we need to store data in Elasticsearch for visualization in Kibana. We will not use a filter as we want to store the tweets in the same way as they are tweeted.

The configuration file will look like this:

```
input {
  twitter {
    consumer_key =>   "XXXXXXXXXXXXXXXXXXX"
    consumer_secret =>   "XXXXXXXXXXXXXXXXXX"
    oauth_token =>   "XXXXXXXXXXXXXXXXXXXXXXXX"
    oauth_token_secret =>   "XXXXXXXXXXXXXXXXXXX"
    keywords => ["#DragMeDownDay,"#BePositive"]
    full_tweet => "true"
  }
}
output {
  elasticsearch {
    protocol => "http"
    host => "localhost"
    port => "9200"
    index => "twitter"
    document_type => "realtime"
  }
}
```

Save this configuration as twitter.conf inside the bin folder of the downloaded Logstash folder.

Let's decode each parameter for better understanding.

Here, input defines an input, which is Twitter. Then, consumer_key, consumer_secret, oauth_token (the access token), and oauth_token_secret (the access secret token) are the credentials needed for the authorization of your application on Twitter, which is done as shown earlier. keywords is used to specify the keywords for which you want to fetch data. In this case, we fetched data about the trending topics on Twitter. All of these parameters are mandatory. The full_tweet parameter, when set to true, specifies that we want to fetch tweets with all fields. Setting it to false would specify Logstash to fetch tweets with limited fields.

Then, we have the following parameters of the output block:

- `output`: This defines the output of the data, which is `elasticsearch`
- `protocol`: This specifies over which protocol the `elasticsearch` instance/server is running
- `host`: This specifies the host address of `elasticsearch`
- `port`: This specifies on which port `elasticsearch` is running
- `index`: This specifies the name of the index in which the fetched data will be stored
- `document_type`: This specifies the type of index

Using the command prompt in Windows or the terminal in Ubuntu, navigate to the `bin` folder inside the Logstash downloaded folder. To run the Logstash configuration, run the following command:

```
logstash agent -f twitter.conf
```

Here, it tells Logstash to start its agent and read the configuration from the `twitter.conf` file.

 Make sure that Elasticsearch is running before you start the Logstash agent. Otherwise, it will give an error.

Upon successful execution of the Logstash agent, the following message will be displayed:

Logstash startup completed

 Before running Logstash, you can check whether your configuration is correct or not using the `logstash agent -f twitter.conf --configtest` command.

Creating visualizations for scenarios

In this section, we will cover the various scenarios described earlier in this chapter, and create visualizations for each scenario. After streaming data into Elasticsearch, we will configure a new index in Kibana and add a Twitter index into it to view the streaming data as covered in *Chapter 1, An Introduction to Kibana*.

Number of tweets over a period of time

In the first scenario, we want to find out how many tweets are being tweeted over a period of time for a particular brand. Using this, a company would come to know the frequency of tweets for its brand over a certain period of time, which makes it easier to view the trend rather than going through huge amounts of raw data. Accordingly, they can monitor the number of tweets for that brand, either for their marketing campaign or to know the popularity of the brand.

To create a visualization for this scenario, we will use a line chart:

- The y axis will have **Count** as the metric
- The x axis will contain the aggregation as the date histogram, followed by the timestamp field with the interval specified in minutes

Now view the visualization by clicking on the **Apply Changes** button, which will be as shown in the following screenshot:

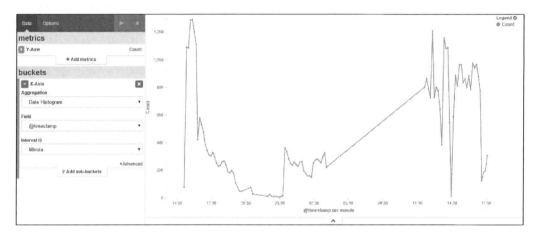

From this, the relevant company can easily monitor the time period when people tweet about them the most, which could help them market their brand or product in specific time periods to get maximum attention. They can also use this as a basic scenario on which they can build up using filters and by digging into the visualization to get more insights. Let's save this visualization as **TweetsperTime**, which we will use to create a dashboard.

Number of tweets in different languages

In our next scenario, we want to find out how many people are tweeting in different languages. This helps the company understand which languages are popular among people tweeting about the company's brand or product.

To create a visualization for this scenario, we will use a vertical bar chart:

1. The *y* axis will have **Count** as the metric.
2. **Split Bars** will contain the aggregation as terms specifying the field as `lang` with the **Top 10** size.
3. Go to the **Options** tab, and select **Bar Mode** as **Grouped** from the drop-down list.

Now view the visualization by clicking on the **Apply Changes** button, which will show you this result:

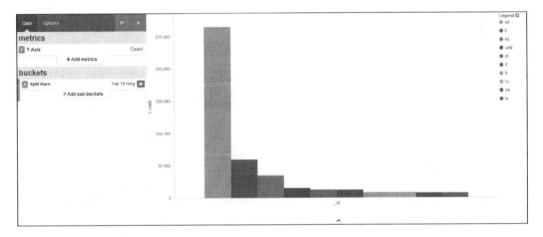

In the preceding screenshot, we compute the top 10 languages in which people are tweeting about a given product or brand. Let's save this visualization as **TopLanguages**, and we will use it to create a dashboard.

Number of tweets from different geographical locations

In this scenario, we want to compute the number of people who are tweeting from different geographical locations. It helps the company understand the geographical location of their existing or prospective customers.

Again, we will use a vertical bar chart to create a visualization for this scenario:

1. The *y* axis will have **Count** as the metric.

2. **Split Bars** will contain the aggregation as terms specifying field as `place.country_code` with the **Top 10** size.

3. Go to the **Options** tab and select **Bar Mode** as **Grouped** from the drop-down list.

Now check out the visualization by clicking on the **Apply Changes** button, which will show you the result like this:

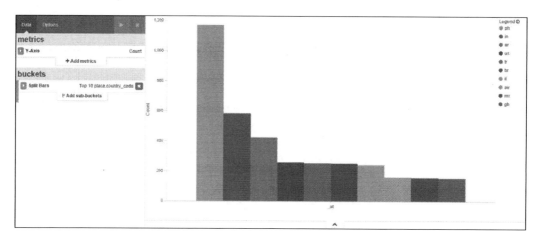

Here, we find out the top 10 geographical locations where people tweet about the product or brand. Let's save this visualization as **TopCountries**, which we will use to create a dashboard.

Sometimes, the field may not show in the Twitter index. To solve this problem, you will need to reload the **Index** field list. This is covered in *Chapter 5, Exploring the Settings Page*, in the *Reloading the index fields list* section.

Number of tweets from Android, iPhone, iPad, and Web devices

In this scenario, we want to find out how many tweets are coming from any of Android, Web, iPhone, and iPad devices over a certain period of time. Using this, the company can come to know which devices drive the brand's maximum traffic on Twitter. Accordingly, they can shape their marketing campaign.

To create a visualization for this scenario, we will use an area chart:

1. The *y* axis will have **Count** as the metric.

2. The *x* axis will contain the aggregation as date histogram, followed by a timestamp field, with the interval specified as hourly.

3. Then we will split the area with the sub-aggregation **Filters**, and specify the filters as `source:android`, `source:iphone OR source:ipad`, and `source:web`.

4. Then we will split the chart with the sub-aggregation **Filters** and specify the same filters. While splitting the chart, we will select the column to split the chart column-wise. Also, the smooth lines box has to be checked.

Now, view the visualization by clicking on the **Apply Changes** button. It will show you the result like this:

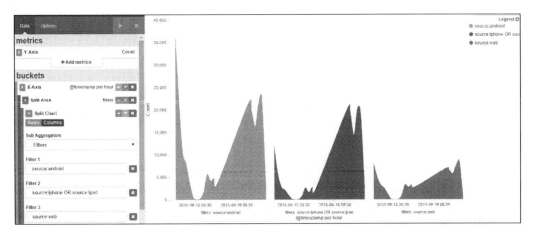

In the preceding screenshot, we can clearly see the comparison of the number of tweets from different devices. Let's save this visualization as **DevicesComparison**. We will use this one as well to create a dashboard.

This scenario can also be used to determine on which platform a company should create its mobile applications. For example, if a company has a website and they want to create an Android, iOS, or Windows mobile application, then using this Twitter analysis, they can figure out on which platform the application should be created. If the company is getting its maximum tweets from Android devices, then they can decide to develop an application for Android.

Number of tweets in various languages using different devices

In our next scenario, we want to compute the number of people who are tweeting in various languages using any Android, Web, iPhone, or iPad devices over a period of time. This helps the company understand which languages are popular among people who tweet about the company brand or product.

To create a visualization for this scenario, we will use an area chart:

1. The *y* axis will have **Count** as the metric.

2. The *x* axis will contain the aggregation as date histogram, followed by a timestamp field, with the interval specified as 3 hours in custom.

3. Then we will split the area with the sub-aggregation as terms, specifying the field as `lang`, with the **Top 5** size.

4. Next, we will split the chart with the sub-aggregation as **Filters**, and specify the filters as `source:android`, `source:iphone OR source:ipad`, and `source:web`.

Now, take a look at the visualization by clicking on the **Apply Changes** button, which will show you the following result:

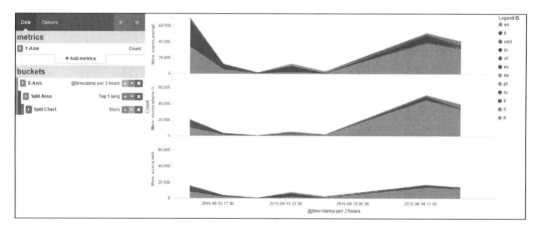

In the preceding screenshot, you can clearly see the comparison of the number of tweets written in various languages using different devices. Let's save this visualization as **DevicesLanguage** for use in our dashboard.

Number of tweets from various countries using different devices

In this scenario, we want to find out how many people are tweeting from various countries using any of Android, Web, iPhone, and iPad devices. This helps companies to understand the demographic locations popular with the brand or product. It also helps them cater to the needs of different countries.

Once again, we will use a vertical bar chart to create a visualization for this scenario:

1. The *y* axis will have **Count** as the metric.
2. The *x* axis will contain the aggregation as terms, specifying the field as `place.country_code` with the **Top 5** size.
3. Then we will split the bars with the sub-aggregation as **Filters**, and specify the filters as `source:android`, `source:iphone OR source:ipad`, and `source:web`.

Now, view the visualization by clicking on the **Apply Changes** button, which will show this result:

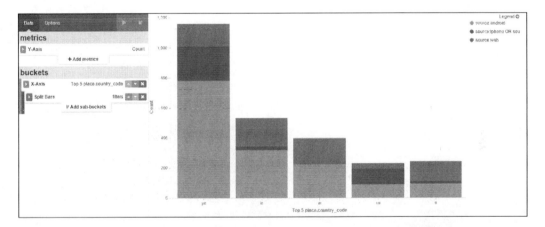

Here, we compute the top five countries from which tweets are made; this is followed by using filters to view tweets from different devices. Let's save this visualization as **DevicesperCountry**, and we will use this one as well to create our dashboard.

The most retweeted user screen name tweeting using different devices

In this scenario, we want to find out what the most popular retweeted user names are for a particular brand. This chart also indicates which devices (Android, Web, iPhone, or iPad) the retweets have been made from. It can be useful for companies to reward users who have been retweeted the most, be it for any marketing campaign or event.

To create a visualization for this scenario, we will use a line chart:

1. The *y* axis will have **Count** as the metric.
2. Split line will contain the aggregation as terms, specifying the field as `retweeted_status.user.screen_name` with the **Top 7** size.
3. The *x* axis will have the sub-aggregation as **Filters**, and we will specify the filters as `source:android`, `source:web`, and `source:iphone OR source:ipad`.

Now, check out the visualization by clicking on the **Apply Changes** button, which will show you this:

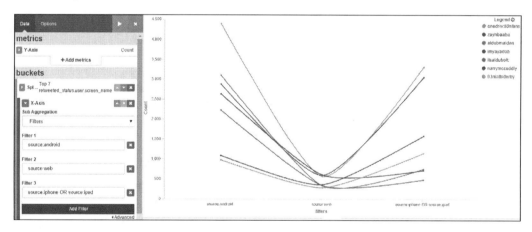

In the preceding screenshot, we have displayed the top seven retweeted user screen names, followed by the different devices used to tweet. Let's save this visualization as **DevicesRetweetCount**, and we will use it to create our dashboard.

Retweeted user screen names indicate that the tweet was retweeted and included the user screen name in the tweet. Also retweeted tweets are indicated by **RT** in the tweet.

The most tweeted user's screen name

In this scenario, we want to compute the top tweeting user's screen name, who has tweeted the most tweets related to the particular brand or product. This can be useful for companies to reward users who have been the most active on Twitter tweeting about their brand, and companies can even surprise their active users with goodies, vouchers, gifts, and so on to engage more people to build their brand.

To create a visualization for this scenario, we will use a pie chart:

1. **Slice Size** will have **Count** as the aggregation.
2. **Split Slices** will contain aggregation as terms, specifying field as `user.screen_name` with the **Top 7** size.

Yet again, you can view the visualization by clicking on the **Apply Changes** button, and this is what you will see:

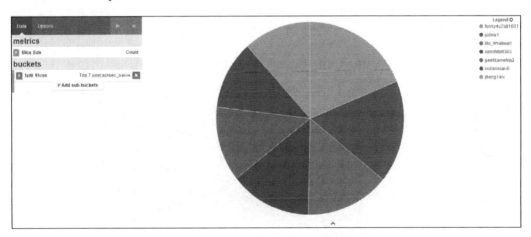

In the preceding screenshot, we have displayed the screen names of the seven people who have tweeted the most. Let's save this visualization as **TopTweetedUsers**, which we will use for our dashboard.

Popular hashtags

In our final scenario, we want to find out the most popular hashtags related to the brand or product. This can be used to find out whether any hashtag related to a product or brand has become popular, with more people tweeting about it. It can also be used by the company to decide whether to use any existing hashtag or decide on a new hashtag for their marketing campaign.

To create a visualization for this scenario, we will use a vertical bar chart:

1. The *y* axis will have **Count** as the metric.
2. The *x* axis will contain the aggregation as date histogram, followed by a timestamp field, with the interval specified as hourly.
3. Then we will split the bars with sub-aggregation as terms, specifying the field as `entities.hashtags.text` with the **Top 5** size.

Now, check out the visualization by clicking on the **Apply Changes** button, which will show you the following result:

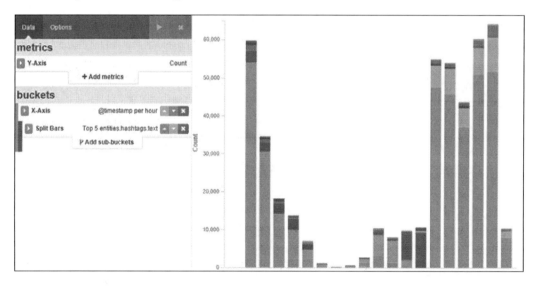

This figure shows the popular hashtags over a period of time related to the company's product or brand.

 The hashtags correspond to the keywords entered in the Logstash configuration file.

Now, before we create a dashboard, let's add another visualization of the **Metrics** type in which we can put all the visualizations as numbers, and it can act as a single view panel to tell us more about the numbers behind the visualizations.

Twitter metrics

In metrics, we will add the following fields corresponding to our scenarios:

- The total count of documents in the index
- The unique count of hashtags used (field: `entities.hashtags.text`)
- The unique count of languages (field: `lang`)
- The unique count of retweeted languages (field: `retweeted_status.user.lang`)
- The unique count of screen names of people who have tweeted (field: `user.screen_name`)
- The unique count of the retweeted status user screen names (field: `retweeted_status.user.screen_name`)
- The unique count of time zones from which people have tweeted (field: `user.time_zone`)
- Percentiles of user favorites count percent of 50, 90, and 99 (field: `user.favourites_count`)
- A percentile rank of 5,000 for the user status count

A dashboard containing all the visualizations created earlier is shown here:

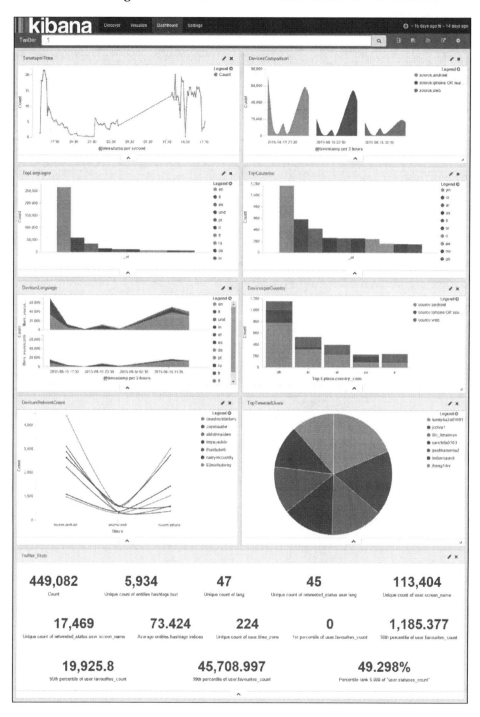

Summary

In this chapter, we covered the basics of Logstash along with the installation of Logstash in Ubuntu and Windows. This was followed by an explanation of the workflow for real-time Twitter data analysis, which included the creation of a Twitter developer account and a Logstash configuration file to fetch tweets. Finally, visualizations were created based on different scenarios and were then combined to form a dashboard.

At the time of writing this book, Kibana is like a baby in the big world of data visualization. The industry has now begun understanding the importance of Kibana, which presents a bright future for this product and its community. With this book, we have tried to provide an unprecedented amount of information about Kibana, covering its installation, the functionality of every component present in it, and how it can be used to attain valuable insights from raw data. We hope that this book becomes a one-stop guide for everyone to learn Kibana. The beautiful journey of doing amazing things with Kibana has just started, so grab this opportunity, have a fun time reading this book, and explore Kibana in a way never done before.

References

This appendix provides a list of links referenced in the book, which are sorted chapter-wise.

Hyperlinks provide a gateway to the extensive literature that can be accessed on the Internet. They provide information above and beyond what one finds in a single article, book, blog, or other media formats. However, when one writes a book, the links provided in the printed book are useful to only those readers who would go to any lengths to find information. For others, these links are irksome, frustrating, and almost useless. They are, of course, useful in online formats, such as e-books.

This appendix is an attempt to provide guidance to the readers. However, some essential information is used in the book in some of the chapters; the links to those are mentioned in the upcoming sections.

Chapter 1, An Introduction to Kibana

- About Kibana: `https://www.elastic.co/products/kibana`
- Official documentation of Kibana v4.1.x: `https://www.elastic.co/guide/en/kibana/4.1/index.html`
- The basic concepts of Elasticsearch: `https://www.elastic.co/guide/en/elasticsearch/reference/current/_basic_concepts.html`
- Official documentation of Elasticsearch v1.5.x: `https://www.elastic.co/guide/en/elasticsearch/reference/1.5/index.html`
- Git for Windows: `https://git-scm.com/`
- Installation of Node.js on various platforms: `https://github.com/nodejs/node-v0.x-archive/wiki/Installing-Node.js-via-package-manager`
- GitHub repository for Kibana: `https://github.com/elastic/kibana`

- GitHub repository for Elasticsearch: `https://github.com/elastic/elasticsearch`
- Usage of elasticdump along with its GitHub Repository: `https://github.com/taskrabbit/elasticsearch-dump`
- Ubuntu community information on Java and its installation: `https://help.ubuntu.com/community/Java`

Chapter 2, Exploring the Discover Page

- A sample tweet explanation: `http://www.scribd.com/doc/30146338/map-of-a-tweet`
- Apache Lucene—query parser syntax: `https://lucene.apache.org/core/2_9_4/queryparsersyntax.html`
- Elasticsearch query string syntax: `https://www.elastic.co/guide/en/elasticsearch/reference/1.5/query-dsl-query-string-query.html#query-string-syntax`
- Elasticsearch string ranges: `https://www.elastic.co/guide/en/elasticsearch/guide/current/_ranges.html`

Chapter 3, Exploring the Visualize Page

- Information about Elasticsearch aggregations: `https://www.elastic.co/guide/en/elasticsearch/reference/1.5/search-aggregations.html`
- Approximate calculations: `https://www.elastic.co/guide/en/elasticsearch/guide/current/_approximate_aggregations.html`
- Elasticsearch scripting: `https://www.elastic.co/guide/en/elasticsearch/reference/1.5/modules-scripting.html`

Chapter 4, Exploring the Dashboard Page

- Official documentation of the Dashboard page: `https://www.elastic.co/guide/en/kibana/4.1/dashboard.html`

Chapter 5, Exploring the Settings Page

- Official documentation of Kibana settings: `https://www.elastic.co/guide/en/kibana/4.1/settings.html`

- Kibana server settings: `https://www.elastic.co/guide/en/kibana/4.1/kibana-server-properties.html`

- Kibana production settings: `https://www.elastic.co/guide/en/kibana/4.1/production.html`

- Official documentation of Numeral.js: `http://numeraljs.com/`

- Managing fields: `https://www.elastic.co/guide/en/kibana/4.1/managing-fields.html`

- Field formatters: `https://www.elastic.co/blog/kibana-4-1-field-formatters`

Chapter 6, Real-Time Twitter Data Analysis

- Official documentation of Logstash: `https://www.elastic.co/guide/en/logstash/1.5/index.html`

- Generating Twitter developer account tokens: `https://dev.twitter.com/oauth/overview/application-owner-access-tokens`

- Twitter input plugin—Logstash: `https://www.elastic.co/guide/en/logstash/1.5/plugins-inputs-twitter.html`

- Input plugins—Logstash: `https://www.elastic.co/guide/en/logstash/1.5/input-plugins.html`

- Filter plugins—Logstash: `https://www.elastic.co/guide/en/logstash/1.5/filter-plugins.html`

- Output plugins—Logstash: `https://www.elastic.co/guide/en/logstash/1.5/output-plugins.html`

- Deprecating Rivers: `https://www.elastic.co/blog/deprecating-rivers`

Index

positive filter
  about 61
  adding 62
primary shard 7
proximity searches 56

Q

query parser syntax, Apache Lucene
  URL 170
query string syntax, Elasticsearch
  URL 170

R

range aggregation 75, 76
Real-Time Twitter data analysis
  workflow 149, 150
refresh interval
  setting 44
regular expressions 57
Remove filter 65
replica shard 8
Representational State Transfer 9
REST API 9, 10

S

sample tweet explanation
  URL 170
Save Dashboard option 117, 118
saved object
  deleting 142
  editing 141
  exporting 142
  importing 142
  viewing 141
Save Search option 58
search bar
  Load Saved Search 59
  New Search 58
  Save Search 58
  using 45-57, 117
Settings page
  about 129
  tabs 129
sharding 7

shards
  primary shard 7
  replica shard 8
significant terms aggregation 77, 78
steps, for designing visualization
  about 81
  search data source, selecting 83, 84
  visualization canvas 84
  visualization type, selecting 82, 83
string ranges, Elasticsearch
  URL 170
String type format
  lower case 135
  short dots 135
  upper case 135
sum aggregation 79

T

tabs, Settings page
  About tab 143
  Advanced tab 138, 139
  Indices tab 129
  Objects tab 140
terms aggregation 77
Tile Map
  about 104
  Desaturate map tiles 108
  Heatmap 107
  Shaded Circle Markers 106
  Shaded GeoHash Grid 106
time filter
  about 38, 39
  setting 39-41
  setting, from histogram 42, 43
Toggle filter 65
TO keyword 49
toolbar
  about 38, 44
  search bar, using 45-57
toolbar, Dashboard page
  about 115
  Add Visualization option 115-117
  Load Saved Dashboard option 118, 119
  New Dashboard option 115
  Save Dashboard option 117, 118
  saved dashboard, loading 118

Thank you for buying
Kibana Essentials

About Packt Publishing

Packt, pronounced 'packed', published its first book, *Mastering phpMyAdmin for Effective MySQL Management*, in April 2004, and subsequently continued to specialize in publishing highly focused books on specific technologies and solutions.

Our books and publications share the experiences of your fellow IT professionals in adapting and customizing today's systems, applications, and frameworks. Our solution-based books give you the knowledge and power to customize the software and technologies you're using to get the job done. Packt books are more specific and less general than the IT books you have seen in the past. Our unique business model allows us to bring you more focused information, giving you more of what you need to know, and less of what you don't.

Packt is a modern yet unique publishing company that focuses on producing quality, cutting-edge books for communities of developers, administrators, and newbies alike. For more information, please visit our website at www.packtpub.com.

About Packt Open Source

In 2010, Packt launched two new brands, Packt Open Source and Packt Enterprise, in order to continue its focus on specialization. This book is part of the Packt Open Source brand, home to books published on software built around open source licenses, and offering information to anybody from advanced developers to budding web designers. The Open Source brand also runs Packt's Open Source Royalty Scheme, by which Packt gives a royalty to each open source project about whose software a book is sold.

Writing for Packt

We welcome all inquiries from people who are interested in authoring. Book proposals should be sent to author@packtpub.com. If your book idea is still at an early stage and you would like to discuss it first before writing a formal book proposal, then please contact us; one of our commissioning editors will get in touch with you.

We're not just looking for published authors; if you have strong technical skills but no writing experience, our experienced editors can help you develop a writing career, or simply get some additional reward for your expertise.

ElasticSearch Cookbook

Second Edition

ISBN: 978-1-78355-483-6   Paperback: 472 pages

Over 130 advanced recipes to search, analyze, deploy, manage, and monitor data effectively with ElasticSearch

1. Deploy and manage simple ElasticSearch nodes as well as complex cluster topologies.

2. Write native plugins to extend the functionalities of ElasticSearch to boost your business.

3. Packed with clear, step-by-step recipes to walk you through the capabilities of ElasticSearch.

Elasticsearch Server

Second Edition

ISBN: 978-1-78398-052-9   Paperback: 428 pages

A practical guide to building fast, scalable, and flexible search solutions with clear and easy-to-understand examples

1. Learn about the fascinating functionalities of ElasticSearch like data indexing, data analysis, and dynamic mapping.

2. Fine-tune ElasticSearch and understand its metrics using its API and available tools, and see how it behaves in complex searches.

3. A hands-on tutorial that walks you through all the features of ElasticSearch in an easy-to-understand way, with examples that will help you become an expert in no time.

Please check **www.PacktPub.com** for information on our titles

Mastering Elasticsearch
Second Edition

ISBN: 978-1-78355-379-2   Paperback: 434 pages

Further your knowledge of the Elasticsearch server by learning more about its internals, querying, and data handling

1. Understand Apache Lucene and Elasticsearch's design and architecture.

2. Design your index, configure it, and distribute it, not only with assumptions, but with the underlying knowledge of how it works.

3. Improve your user search experience with Elasticsearch functionality and learn how to develop your own Elasticsearch plugins.

Building a Search Server with Elasticsearch [Video]

ISBN: 978-1-78328-415-3   Duration: 01:53 hours

Build a fully featured and scalable search UI with Elasticsearch

1. Start building your own search engine with Elasticsearch, from setup to ingestion and querying.

2. Set up an Elasticsearch cluster and a full search interface in AngularJS, all in one comprehensive project.

3. Implement search features such as highlighting, filters, and autocomplete, and build a robust search engine.

Made in the USA
Lexington, KY
05 April 2016